Life Topics

Reflections

by
Jonathan Berman
Takashi Shimaoka

音声ファイル
無料 DL
のご案内

このテキストの音声を無料で視聴（ストリーミング）・ダウンロードできます。自習用音声としてご活用ください。
以下のサイトにアクセスしてテキスト番号で検索してください。

https://nanun-do.com　テキスト番号［**511966**］

※ 無線 LAN（WiFi）に接続してのご利用を推奨いたします。

※ 音声ダウンロードは Zip ファイルでの提供になります。
お使いの機器によっては別途ソフトウェア（アプリケーション）の導入が必要となります。

※ Life Topics: Reflections 音声ダウンロードページは以下の QR コードからもご利用になれます。

This book is dedicated to you, the students,
without whose help it would not have been possible.

Life Topics
Reflections

* Ideal for classwork in Reading, Writing, Conversation, Presentation, Debate.
* Emphasizes Creative and Critical Thinking skills.
* Designed for a wide range of students. Lower-level students benefit from simple, natural English. Advanced students gain from a greater range and depth of ideas.
* Includes thought-provoking issues that are fun, relevant, and meaningful.
* Encourages passionate classroom discussions and inspiring classroom experiences.
* Explores many sides of important social and personal topics.
* Enhances students' self-awareness and understanding of their environment to help prepare them for life.
* Comes with an Internet page at http://www.LifeTopics.com

"Education is not the filling of a pail, but the lighting of a fire."

– ***William Butler Yeats***

Table of Contents

1. Cat Café

Pre-Reading Question: When and where did the first cat café begin?

Vocabulary: Match the words with their meanings or descriptions.

1. companionship 交わり	2. cuddle 寄り添う	3. judge 判断する
4. self-esteem 自尊心	5. sociable 社交的な	6. themes テーマ、主題

____ a. a feeling of friendship

____ b. one's confidence or self-worth

____ c. to criticize another person

____ d. to hold, hug, or embrace

____ e. different topics or main ideas

____ f. friendly and getting along well with others

Vocabulary: Fill in the blanks in the sentences below with the correct word.

A. Before you ________ another person, you should look carefully at yourself.
B. The lecture went so well, that after she gave it, her ________ went up.
C. The talk covered different ________, including world peace and hope.
D. He was very talkative and far more ________ than the others.
E. A dog can provide its owner with ________ for many years.
F. My daughter loves to ________ with her cat, Smoky.

CD 2

"Every problem has a gift for you in its hands."
– Richard Bach

[1] The world's first cat café, called the "Cat Flower Garden," opened in 1998 in Taiwan. It soon became famous, attracting tourists from Japan and around the world. In 2004, Osaka opened Japan's first cat café, called "Neko no Jikan" (Cat's Time), and a year later, Tokyo opened its first cat café. Perhaps because so many apartments do not allow pets, cat cafés spread quickly and became very popular throughout the country. Japan soon became well known for its cat cafés which served coffee, tea, and cake, cookies, and other small sweets. Most cafés had from 10 to 20 cats, for people to pet and play with. Customers, often businessmen, go to these places to relax, find **companionship**, and forget about their work and stress for a while.

[2] People love their pets. A 2011 study found that pet owners are happier, healthier, more **sociable**, and have higher **self-esteem**. Today, cat cafés operate throughout Asia, including in Singapore, Taiwan, and Thailand. In 2011 they appeared in Russia, and in 2014 they emerged in Europe. They were found first in Italy, Denmark, and Finland, and later in Germany, the Netherlands, Poland, France, and England. In 2014, Canada

also opened its first cat café in Montreal, and that same year, cat cafés opened in California and Florida. Since then, they have spread across the U.S. Today, many other types of animals can now be found in "pet cafés," including dogs, birds, rabbits, owls, or even goats. Many cafés encourage customers to adopt their animals.

[3] The pet café trend has led to some exciting trends. At one university in London, students can **cuddle** with rabbits on Fridays. "Rabbits don't **judge** you on what you wear or what grade you got on your last assignment. They just want to cuddle," said one student. About a hundred students visit their cute, long-eared friends weekly, with some visitors saying it is the best part of their week. Another university in England has "puppy rooms" to help students handle the stress of exams.

[4] Different café **themes** are becoming popular. At hammock cafés customers spend their time relaxing on hammocks. In chocolate cafés, they can choose from among many different chocolate treats. There are different anime themes too, like Gundam, Snoopy, and Super Mario, as well as themes such as Hello Kitty and Barbie dolls, robots, and ninjas. London has one place with over one hundred breakfast cereals from around the world. Some cafés are decorated to look like cafés from the 1950s, with designs, tables, chairs, and wall pictures that bring back those years. Other cafés have movie-related themes as "Back to the Future" and "Alien." So, if you're in the mood for a "different" café experience, you have all kinds of great choices.

"A pessimist sees the difficulty in every opportunity; an optimist sees the opportunity in every difficulty."

– Winston Churchill

Active Outline: Choose the correct answer.

1. The world's first cat café opened in __________. (Japan / Taiwan / The UK / America)
   a. Before long, they quickly spread throughout __________.
   (Japan / Taiwan / The UK / America)
2. Studies have found that pet owners are generally healthier and happier. (True / False)
   a. Cat cafés became popular in Europe and the US beginning in __________.
   (2004 / 2005 / 2014 / 2015)
3. At one university in England, students can spend time with rabbits on __________.
   (Mondays / Wednesdays / Fridays / weekends)
4. Which is **not** mentioned as a theme for a café? (Gundam / Barbie / robots / fish)

Creative Writing I: Review an animal or pet café. *Be creative, and use your imagination!!*

While in the (country / city / town / __________) of __________, I visited a (cat / dog / __________) café that had just opened. When I opened the door, there were__________ (cats / dogs / __________ that (ran / flew / came / __________) to me. The room was very __________, and I noticed that the walls had __________ __________ on them. The animals had many interesting names, such as __________, __________, and __________, and while some were playing with __________, others were resting and __________ on chairs or __________

__________. The other customers there looked __________
__________.
The animals were __________. The cutest one, named __________, suddenly

_______________ and began to _______________ and _______________. It remained there for _____________ minute(s), and after that started to _______________ _______________________________. In addition, there was _______________ that was ____________. It's a _______________ way to spend your time and ____. Before I left, I decided to buy (a / some) ____. The one thing that I think can make the place better is ____.
In the future, I (will / will not) return because ____
____.

Reverse Questions: Write the questions that you would need to ask to get the answers below.

1. ____?

   Answer: It was called "Neko no Jikan."

2. ____?

   Answer: They first appeared in 2014 in California and Florida.

3. ____?

   Answer: Cuddling with rabbits and puppy rooms help students handle stress.

4. ____?

   Answer: Some café themes today might include ice cream, baseball, and "Star Wars."

Discussion: (Answer a couple of these).

I. Whom do you know who has a pet? Describe the animal, and the feelings towards it.

   One person I know who (has / had) a pet is _______________. The pet (is / was) a _______________, named _______________, and looks like _______________. The feeling toward the animal are ____
   ____.

II. Can a pet be considered part of the family? Explain.

   I (do / do not) feel that a pet can be part of the family because _______________
   ____
   ____.

III. Many people go to cat cafés to relax. Where do you go to relax?

   Outside of my home, a place I go to relax is _______________________. While I am there I will ____
   ____
   ____.

IV. Which would you prefer to go to, a "Star Wars," baseball, or ice cream café? Why?

   I would prefer to go to a ("Star Wars" / baseball / ice cream café) because
   ____
   ____.

Creative Writing II: Create your own "pet or themed café."

After much thought, I have decided to create my own café. But it will not have cats. It will have (animals as / the theme of) ______________. I like this idea because ____. This café will appeal to many people because ____.

The name of the café will be ________________. It will be located in ______________. This is a good location because ______________________________. In the middle of the café will be a large ______________. It will be ______________ in color. The nicest part of the café will be ______________________________. The inside of the café will also have ______________________________ and ______________________________. The price to enter the café will be ______________. In addition, if people like, they can buy ______________ and ______________________________.

My Feedback: Give feedback and write down some questions to ask the speakers.

______________________________? ______________________________?

______________________________? ______________________________?

Conversation / Debate: Answer a couple of these questions, and discuss them with your classmates.

I. Describe your favorite café. Why do you like it?

II. What special-themed café would you like to go to (such as an owl or Gundam café, etc.) Why?

III. Do you believe that pet owners are really happier, healthier, and more sociable than people who do not own pets? Explain.

IV. If your university had a pet café, what animals would you like to see there? Would you visit it? Explain. If not, why not?

Make up two questions of your own to discuss with the other class members. Be creative !!

2. Sad Songs

Pre-Reading Question: Can sad songs make us happy? Why or why not?

Vocabulary: Match the words with their meanings or descriptions.

1. chills 寒気	2. cope with 対抗する	3. empathy 共感	4. journey 旅
5. overcame 乗り越える	6. nostalgic 郷愁に満ちた	7. substance 物質	

____ a. a trip
____ b. a type of material
____ c. successfully dealt with
____ d. remembering something from the past
____ e. understanding the feelings of others
____ f. a happy shudder; thrill
____ g. to calmly deal with concerns or problems

Vocabulary: Fill in the blanks in the paragraph below with the correct word.

I often listen to music to better (a) __________ the stresses of college study and life. I wonder if my brain releases a (b) __________ to make me feel this way. Often, my mind takes me on a (c) __________ of feelings and memories, both good and bad. Sometimes, I remember a time when I (d) __________ some past difficulties, and other times, I just get (e) __________ and (f) __________ thinking about the "good old days." If the song is about difficult times, my (g) __________ increases.

CD 3

"If music be the food of love, play on."
– William Shakespeare

[1] People in every country of the world have music. Babies as young as five months old, even before they learn to walk or talk, can tell the difference between an upbeat song and a sadder one. As we listen to music, the mind releases a feel-good **substance** that makes us relax. It can actually cause **chills**. Anyone who loves music knows that music affects our behavior and emotions. Out of all the different types of music, sad music probably has the greatest effect on us.

[2] Sad songs often makes us **nostalgic**, reminding us of a distant time and place. Perhaps, we remember a time when things were a bit better, when we were a little happier, or a time when we **overcame** difficult challenges. Perhaps the music reminds us of past relationships. We often remember a happy or a sad emotion, or an emotion that is both happy and sad (such as when a pet that we loved dies). By listening to others who have had similar experiences as ours, we can better understand the music and better connect with their emotions, which increases our **empathy**. Sad music has certain soothing qualities, in that when we listen to music about lives that are sadder than our own life, we feel that things are not so bad. This results in "peaceful" feelings and positive emotions that help us better handle our own emotional problems.

[3] While no one likes being sad, when we are in a bad mood, most people prefer sad songs to happy songs. This might seem strange, since sadness is an emotion that most of us want to avoid. But if we always wanted to avoid sadness, no one would listen to sad music. While listening to sad songs, we often remember sad, romantic, or unpleasant feelings that we have had or have, but explore them in a safe way. This can help us to better handle our emotions. People listen to sad songs after a break-up, or after an argument with someone they care for, or when they are feeling lonely or homesick.

[4] When a person relates to a sad song, he/she shares the experiences of loss, difficulty, or unanswered love mentioned in the song. When we have no one to talk to, sad songs can actually help us better **cope with** the negative or unwanted emotions of daily life. Music has a way of talking to us, of taking us on a **journey** that can move us emotionally to a healthier place.

They reach into your room
Just feel their gentle touch
When all hope is gone
Sad songs say so much

– Elton John, Sad Songs, 1984

Active Outline: Choose the correct answer.

1. Music can actually give us chills. (True / False)
2. Sad songs remind us of past experiences. (True / False)

   a. When listening to a sad song, we often feel __________ about ourself. (better / sadder)
3. When we are in a bad mood, we prefer __________ songs. (happy / sad)
4. While we listen to sad songs, we often remember __________ feelings of our own. (similar / different)

   a. Sad music can take us on ___ ____. (an emotional journey / a fun trip)

Comprehension:

Name three songs that give you strong emotions.

The Song's Name:	What feelings do you get from the song?
1. ____________________	______________________________
2. ____________________	______________________________
3. ____________________	______________________________

Writing:

1. How do you cope with bad days (other than by listening to music)?

   When I have a bad day, to make myself feel better I will often ______________________ *or* ______________________________________ *. For example, when* ______________________________________ *. What happened was* ______________________________________ ______________________________________ *.*

2. What music do you listen to when you're not in a good mood?

   One song I listen to when I'm not in a good mood is ______________________ *. For example, there was a time when* ______________________________________ ______________________________________ *.*

3. What music do you listen to to get motivated?

   A song I listen to to get motivated is ______________________ *. For example, one time,* ______________________________________ *.*

Memories:

Our favorite songs often remind us of a different place and time that, perhaps, we haven't told anyone about. Name two songs, and then explain what they remind you of.

Song's Name:	**What does it remind you of?**
Ex: *"Let It Be" by The Beatles*	*I remember the first time I danced with my girlfriend to this song. What happened was ... .*
1. ______________________	______________________________________ ______________________________________ ______________________________________
2. ______________________	______________________________________ ______________________________________ ______________________________________

Sentence Completion: Based on today's reading, fill in the blanks to complete the sentences.

1. It is ______________________ who can tell the difference between happy and sad songs, and they know it before they can even ______________ or ______________.
2. It is ______________ songs that most affects our emotions and that can take us to another time and ______________.
3. By ______________________________ sad songs, we often feel that things in our own life are not so bad, and we can feel ______________ emotions.
4. Although people usually try to avoid sadness, interestingly, they prefer ____________________ to ______________ songs.
5. Sad songs can help us better deal with unwanted ______________.

Creative Writing: Tell your classmates about a musical experience you have had. *Be creative, and use your imagination!!*

It was last summer that I went to see my favorite band. The band's name is ____________. I went with my three best friends named ____________, ____________, and ____________. Once at the concert, I became hungry, and saw the most delicious-looking ____________ ever. When I tried it, it tasted ____________. I shared the food with my friends, and we noticed that everyone was having a great time, singing, dancing, and ______ing. The weather outside was ____________________; however, there was still a bit of ____________. I was ____________, and I then noticed that a member of the band was looking at me, and he smiled. He then called me up on the stage! I was so ____________, (and / but) decided to go. Once I was on stage, he handed me his ______________ and asked me to play. Although I had never played an instrument before, I played it. It sounded ________________________. Everyone in the audience heard me play, and they were ________________________ and ________________________. What I remember most about being on stage was ____. ____. Whenever I hear the song named ____, I remember that very special day.

My Feedback: Give feedback and write down some questions to ask the speakers.

______________________________? ______________________________?

______________________________? ______________________________?

Opinion: Discuss the speakers' stories with your classmates. Who was most creative? Why?

Discussion:

Describe the best live band or concert you have ever seen. Who did you go with? Where and when was it? Offer additional interesting details about what happened.

Debate: Do you think that sad music can make you feel better? Why or why not? Discuss this question with your classmates.

Make up two questions of your own to discuss with the other class members. Be creative !!

3. The History of Consumerism

Pre-Reading Question: Give examples of how shopping has changed in the past 100 years.

Vocabulary: Match the words and phrases in bold with their endings.

1. control demand 需要を制御する　2. consumer culture 消費者文化　3. defined 定義する
4. overwhelmed 圧倒する　5. status 地位　6. store credit 支払ったお金を返金せずお店に預けておくこと

1. The people **control demand**. ____ a. an economy based on buying and selling goods
2. America is a **consumer culture**. ____ b. to have too much of something
3. He is **defined** by his clothing. ____ c. decides how much is bought and sold
4. He is **overwhelmed** with so much stuff. ____ d. selling goods without immediate payment
5. She buys costly things to improve her **status**. ____ e. to express or describe
6. The store gave **store credit** to its customers. ____ f. importance; position

Vocabulary: Fill in the blanks in the paragraph below with the correct word.

It is (a) ______ that has, in many ways, (b) ______ American culture. Americans love to buy things. Often, new, expensive goods show a person's (c) ______. It is the people who (d) ______, and if a store does not sell the goods that people want, the store will go out of business. With the creation of (e) ______, things became much easier for consumers to get. Eventually, however, people bought so much "stuff" that they were (f) ______ by all their goods.

CD 4

"Every generation laughs at the old fashions, but religiously follows the now."
– Henry David Thoreau

[1] Much of American society was by and large created for the selling and buying of goods. For this reason, it can be called a **consumer culture**. A person's **status** is often measured by what he/she owns. Early consumerism theory stated that consumers **control demand**. It is a simple idea that suggests that buying more stuff is good for people and helps the economy. Before the invention of electricity and the rise of the factory, consumerism was difficult. People had few options. For most people, goods were only available at the local store and too expensive. Many goods were only accessible to the wealthy.

[2] In America, the idea of **store credit**, or "buy now, pay later," began around the 1920s; by the 1940s, it was common to buy things on credit. In the 1950s, incomes increased, and so did people's desire to buy stuff. This meant buying a large, new home, and filling it with a new refrigerator, vacuum cleaner, washing machine, stove, radio, television, and everything else. Large, attractive department stores emerged, promising a luxurious shopping experience and urging people to buy at "discount" prices. A new trend began: keeping up with what your neighbors had and buying not what was needed, but what was wanted. Soon came the introduction of the credit card, which further encouraged consumers to buy and spend more by allowing them to purchase almost anything – with money that did not actually exist.

[3] In the 1960s, shopping centers that appealed to every member of the family became increasingly common. Cheap goods were available everywhere, and people **defined** themselves not so much by what they were, but rather by what they owned. By the 1970s, shopping centers and retail outlets grew, and America became a full consumer culture. Americans were shopping and spending as much as four times more than Europeans. Shopping not only involved the purchasing of essential goods, it also meant engaging in fun activities. Shopping malls joined with other entertainments such as movie theaters, restaurants, night clubs, and arcades, to offer everyone an enjoyable afternoon or evening out.

[4] When the 1980s began, people felt that they had to buy more stuff, "live large," and spend lots of money, usually on their credit card. Shopping grew at a rapid pace, as there were far more choices than ever before. Malls became bigger and were everywhere, selling everything imaginable: early video games, electronics, accessories, clothing, and many other products. In the 1990s, people "upgraded" to goods that looked better, used less electricity, and caused less pollution. They also upgraded because they saw their friends and neighbors doing it. Buying more goods than ever before, many people were **overwhelmed** by everything they owned.

[5] As the 2000s began, everyone had to have the newest electronic gadget – perhaps best represented by the iPod and smart phone – which offered new ways to listen to music, watch television, and socialize. The Internet grew, and so did online shopping. Shopping became almost effortless, as you could comfortably sit at home and purchase anything at all, any hour of the day or night, from around the world. Many shopping malls and regular stores went out of business because they had difficulty selling their goods, as online retailers and individuals were selling the same items more cheaply.

"We buy things we don't need, with money we don't have, to impress people we don't like."

– Fight Club

Active Outline: Choose the correct answer.

1. Early consumerism said that it's the ________ who affects how much is sold. (buyer / seller)
   a. Back then, buying things was ________ difficult. (very / not)
2. Keeping up with your neighbors meant that people bought ________. (more / less)
3. In the 1970s, ________ became more of a consumer culture. (America / Europe)
4. Many items became more energy efficient during the ________. (1970s / 1980s / 1990s)
5. In the 2000s, ________ grew most quickly. (shopping malls / credit cards / the Internet)
   a. A major product that represented the 2000s was the ________. (car / iPod / clothes / radio)

Discussion:

Name two items that you buy at malls or stores, or used or secondhand, or at outdoor markets, or online.

Malls or stores:	1. ________	2. ________
Used or secondhand items:	1. ________	2. ________
Outdoor markets or festivals:	1. ________	2. ________
Internet:	1. ________	2. ________

Opinion: Describe your overall shopping habits.

Sequence Order: Number the sentences below in the correct order as explained in the reading.

_9_ a. Malls were everywhere, and people bought early video games.
____ b. The beginning of store credit, which allowed people to shop using credit at certain stores.
____ c. Every new home had to have a new refrigerator, washing machine, television, etc.
____ d. People "upgraded" their appliances and devices to ones that saved energy.
____ e. The rise of factories and electricity made many goods very cheap.
____ f. People began to express themselves by what they owned.
____ g. The credit card was first introduced.
____ h. Online shopping grew with the Internet, and everyone wanted the newest electronic gadget.
_1_ i. Most goods were available to the wealthy only.
____ j. Shopping malls combined with different entertainment to give people an enjoyable time out.
____ k. Large department stores had opened for the first time.

Creative Thinking: Individual Work. Make an advertisement for some device, appliance, or other item found inside the home.

1. What is the item? Give it a name. (Ex: *This is Sammy the Cool Refrigerator*).
   The item is a ____________________. *Its name is* ____________________.
2. Describe the item.
   It is the color ____________________ *and has* ____________________.
   Its (size / shape) are ____________________.
3. Draw a picture of it.
   Here is the item ____________________.
   Here people are using it ____________________.
   And here I am ____________________.

Creative Thinking: Group Work. Everyone in the group is president of a company that has developed a new product. To sell your product, you must write an effective advertisement for it.

1. What are you selling? *The item we are selling is a / an* ____________________.
2. Give it a name. *Its name is* ____________________.
3. Describe the item.
   It is the color __________ *with* __________. *Its size and shape are* __________.
   What makes it look unusual is that ____________________.
4. Give the item some unusual power. (Ex: *The washing machine cleans clothes while you wear them!*)
   What the unusual power of this item is ____________________.

5. Create a slogan. Note: Slogans should be creative and fun, not literal. (Ex: *This Refrigerator Keeps Food Cold* --- is a terrible slogan). ______________________________.
6. Create a television commercial for your product. The commercial must include all of the above information. Be prepared to act the commercial out in front of the class.

   Notes: ____

   ____

   ____.

Matching: Based on today's reading, match the sentence beginnings and endings.

1. Before the credit card became common ____ A. to spend more money.
2. We are now buying more ____ B. but bought what they wanted.
3. The credit card encourages people ____ C. without leaving the home.
4. People no longer bought what they needed, ____ D. by the newest electronic gadgets.
5. The 2000s can be best represented ____ E. people bought stuff using store credit.
6. Now we can shop anytime, day or night, ____ F. and more goods than ever before.

Creative Writing: Describe going on a fun shopping trip. *Be creative, and use your imagination!!*

I decided to take a trip shopping far away, and to do something fun. To get there, I took a __________ and then a __________ to get to the (city / country / __________) of __________. When I first arrived, I saw a park, and it had a large __________. Then, I came upon a (temple / statue / __________) with many people there who were __________. There was a festival, and I saw some fruit for sale, so I decided to eat (a / an) __________, and it tasted __________. The music was loud, and the band (played / didn't play) well. There were __________ made by hand for sale that would make a perfect gift for my __________.

Ahead of me, there was a large (castle / garden / __________) and lots of trees, across from a small river. While crossing it, I saw lots of __________ and __________, and I heard the sounds of __________. Eventually, I arrived at a place that sold large paintings of colored (dragons / butterflies / __________). There was also an old woman selling things. She looked at me, and handed me something and told me to open it. It was shaped like a __________ and it smelled like __________. After I opened it, I noticed something strange inside. It looked (round / square / __________) with __________.
I was so surprised when I saw that __________

__________.

My Feedback: Give feedback and write down some questions to ask the speakers.

______________________? ______________________?
______________________? ______________________?

Make up two questions of your own to discuss with the other class members. Be creative !!

4. A Sense of Purpose

Pre-Reading Question: How important is having a sense of purpose in life? Why?

Vocabulary: Fill in the blanks in the paragraph below with the correct word.

1. the big picture 大局	2. confidence 自信	3. donate 寄付する
4. flexible 柔軟な	5. inspiration 刺激	6. meaningful relationships 有意義な関係
7. psychological 心理的な		

We often assume that to (a) ______ our time to helping others would not be enjoyable. This is untrue. When we look at (b) ______, we find that helping others usually motivates us, leading to (c) ______ and other wonderful things, including an increase of (d) ______ within ourselves. This can work as long as we are (e) ______. There are also other (f) ______ reasons why helping others is good for us. It allows us to meet interesting people, and can even lead to (g) ______.

CD 5

"Your purpose in life is to find your purpose and give your whole heart and soul to it."

– The Buddha

[1] Unlike other animals, humans need to have a strong sense of purpose. Having a purpose in life can determine who we are, our energy level, and even our life force. It can make us feel alive and help create a life worth living. It can give us a greater chance to have more friends and **meaningful relationships**. Doctors know how important diet and exercise are for good health. But some also believe that having a sense of purpose is just as important – that it can even add years to our lives.

[2] People with purpose have a reason to wake up in the morning. They have greater **confidence** and focus, and they can be an **inspiration** to others. Even after a bad day, purpose helps people feel better more quickly. Mentally, people with purpose are stronger, less likely to be bored, stressed, or depressed, or to have other **psychological** difficulties. Physically they are healthier, too, less likely to have a stroke, heart attack, or other serious disease.

[3] To achieve greater meaning and joy, people all across the globe **donate** their time, doing things that are important to them to help make the world a better place – to become a part of something larger than themselves. College graduates these days are now more likely to seek jobs with purpose; for some, finding a meaningful job is more important than earning a big salary. But a sense of purpose should involve something more than just a job. People who fulfill their purpose only through their work will have a hard time when they leave their job. People who retire young, say at age of 55, are more likely to die younger than those who retire at 65. This is often because once their career ends, their purpose in life also ends because they had no strong goals outside of work. They connected their sense of purpose to what they did, instead of to who they are.

[4] Only you can find your sense of purpose. We start to realize and think about this in high school or college. It does not matter when we find our purpose, whether it is in our 20s, 40s, or even 70s. It can be as simple as making others around you happy, doing well at school or work, or doing something fun or creative as part of a circle, or anything at all. To find your purpose, it is important to get out of your usual daily routine, take a step back, and look at **the big picture** of your life.

[5] Many people assume that there is only one purpose in life. They struggle to find what that single perfect purpose is, which they also see as a part of a perfect future. This is a mistake. There is no single life plan for anyone. Things can change, and quickly. So you must be **flexible**, since there will be changes that you have no control over. Get comfortable with having different purposes, even at the same time, since change always happens. At all times be curious, learn, experiment, get new information. Talk with people who can encourage you. Ask yourself questions. Find your strengths and develop them to their fullest. Ask yourself, what do I care about? What gets me excited? What brings me joy? What are my passions? What gives my life meaning? Perhaps there is no perfect you; but a better you is always possible.

"Life is never made unbearable by circumstance, but only by a lack of meaning and purpose."
– Viktor Frankl

Active Outline: Choose the correct answer.

1. A sense of purpose can ________. (increase our energy level / make us feel more alive / Neither of these. / Both of these.)
   a. Having a sense of purpose can add ________ to your life. (days / months / years)
2. People with a sense of purpose are more likely to be ________ healthier. (physically / mentally / Both of these. / Neither of these.)
3. Many college graduates today are more likely ________ look for a job with purpose. (to / not to)
   a. A person's sense of purpose should only be found through his or her job. (True / False)
4. Most people find their sense of purpose while they are in college. (True / False)
5. It is important to look for a single, perfect purpose in life. (True / False)
   a. It is important to assume that things always change, and that you should change, too. (True / False)
   b. To find your sense of purpose, it ________ important to be curious, to look at your strengths, and to ask yourself what gives you joy. (is / is not)

Creative Discussion:

What is one thing you hate – that is definitely **not** your sense of purpose? Now, discuss this thing with your classmates **as if it were** your sense of purpose. For example, you might speak positively about playing with cockroaches, or breaking an arm, or swimming with sharks, or studying for the TOEFL. But make sure it's something you have no interest in – but talk as if you love it!

Think of two things that are **not** part of your sense of purpose and write them here.

1. ______________________ 2. ______________________

A. Choose one of the above.

B. Make up a "pretend" story about why you love it so much. Write about how much this "loved" activity gives you a sense of purpose. Use expressive words. ***Be sarcastic, creative - and funny!***

Notes: ____

____

____

____.

Discussion Activity:

Now discuss your story with a partner, and, if possible, present it to the class. Describe how you felt and what happened while you were doing this activity.

Sentence Unscramble:

Put the words in the correct order to make complete sentences.

1. other animals, / humans / should have / purpose. / a sense of / Unlike

____

2. important / diet and / think that having purpose / Some doctors / exercise. / as / is as

____

3. bad day, / Even / more quickly. / recover emotionally / can / after a / people with purpose

____

4. to / place. / People with / make / the world / a better / their time / purpose donate

____

5. purpose / can find / any age. / People / at / their

____

6. and think / a step back, / about / want / Take / to go. / where you

____

7. as / as / making / purpose in life / simple / others happy. / One's / can be

____

8. have not / but many / purposes. / different / person should / A / just one,

____

9. you / you. / Perhaps / a / better / can / create

____

Writing / Conversation:

Name three things that you did back in high school or middle school that really mattered to you.

A. ______________ B. ______________ C. ______________

Opinion: Choose one of the above and describe it in detail. Why was it so important to you?

Of the above, I enjoyed ______________. What happened was ______________ ______________. The reason it was so important was because ______________.

Critical Thinking: What is one thing that you currently care deeply about? ______________

What do you like about it?

1. ______________
2. ______________
3. ______________

What is difficult about it?

1. ______________
2. ______________
3. ______________

Opinion: What can you do to help improve the thing that matters to you?

Group Discussion: Give feedback on what you liked about each speaker's ideas. Write down some questions to ask the speaker.

______________ ______________

______________ ______________

Creative / Critical Thinking: What are three accomplishments that you achieved? Write a creative sentence to describe each one, as in the example.

What I accomplished:	Creative Sentence:
Ex: *The day I swam 200 meters.*	*"I felt like a dolphin."*
1. ______________	" ______________."
2. ______________	" ______________."
3. ______________	" ______________."

Opinion: Choose one of the accomplishments you wrote about above. What would you change about it to make it better? Explain.

Debate: On a scale of 1-10, how important is it to have sense of purpose in life? Explain and discuss.

Make up two questions of your own to discuss with the other class members. Be creative !!

5. Santa Claus

Pre-Reading Question: What is the history of Santa Claus?

Vocabulary: Fill in the blanks in the sentences below with the correct word.

1. chimneys 煙突	2. elf 妖精	3. elves 妖精（複数）
4. fur trim 毛皮の飾り付きの	5. huge feasts 盛大な祝宴	6. nodded 頷く
7. puppet 操り人形	8. sleigh そり	9. sneaky こっそりとする
10. statue 像		

A. The house has not one but two ______. B. There were ______ to celebrate the holidays.

C. The ______ went down the hill very fast. D. The plural of ______ is ______.

E. There was a large ______ made of stone in the middle of the park.

F. She ______ her head yes, but her eyes told him that she was up to something ______.

G. The man entertained us with a small ______ that wore a red jacket with white ______.

CD 6

[1] The story of Santa Claus began with a man named St. Nicholas in around the year 280 A.D. Nicholas lived in what is now Turkey. His parents had died when he was a child, but they had had lots of money, so he suddenly found himself very wealthy. He decided to travel across the land, and, being very kind, in time he began giving all of his wealth away. He gave gifts to everybody, especially children, and became extremely popular. Nicholas died on December 6, and even today, the anniversary of his death is celebrated with **huge feasts**, and is considered lucky for people when they buy expensive items or get married.

[2] In America, the name Santa Claus came from the word "Sinter Klaas," which is the Dutch name for St. Nicholas. In 1774, a newspaper in New York wrote about all the people who celebrated his death, called St. Nicholas Day. In 1809, a book came out that told the story of how Sinter Klaas, or St. Nicholas, was actually living in New York. The book claimed that he was fat, smoked a pipe, and wore a large green jacket to keep warm. He became even more popular and was described as everything from being rather **sneaky** to wearing a yellow stocking and a blue triangle-shaped hat. In 1822, a minister wrote a poem for his children called *The Night Before Christmas* in which Santa Claus was said to be as small as an **elf**, cheerful, and fat. He had a **sleigh** with bells that was pulled by reindeer and climbed **chimneys** when Santa **nodded** his head.

[3] By the 1840s, to encourage Christmas shopping, stores began displaying pictures of Santa Claus. In 1841 thousands of people visited Philadelphia to see the new **statue** of Santa Claus there. In the 1860s, a magazine named *Harper's Weekly* included many drawings of Santa who, for the first time, was a fat, cheerful man with a large, white beard, bright red suit with white **fur trim** and a large black belt with a large buckle. Santa could slide down chimneys, and, at times, was even wearing an American Flag. He was also married to Mrs. Claus, lived near the North Pole, had a workshop where **elves** made toys for children, and sometimes used a **puppet** named "Jeff." The idea of Santa Claus appearing in person in department stores began in 1890 in Massachusetts, where mall workers dressed as Santa and others as elves who would make small toys and give them to children. In 1897, a newspaper called *The New York Sun* asked, "Is there a Santa Claus?" and answered with a "Yes, ... there is!" This made Santa a legend throughout America and Canada. His appearance changed, at times he was short and other times tall, even as big as a giant. He wore suits that were blue, red, brown, green, purple, or gold.

[4] By 1920, however, the most popular Santa Claus had a red suit with white fur trim and a large black belt. At Christmas, stores were using Santa to advertise and sell all their goods. Beginning in 1931, Coca-Cola used this picture of Santa to increase the sales of their soft drink during the winter season. All this advertising helped create the standard image of Santa that we know today. Santa had become more commercial than religious. In 1934, the song "Santa Claus is Coming to Town" became a big hit. It told of how Santa made a list of "naughty or nice" children throughout the world. So, if you wanted to get a present from Santa, you "had better be nice."

"Creativity is intelligence having fun."
– Albert Einstein

Active Outline: Choose the correct answer.

1. St. Nicholas was known as a very __________ person. (generous / funny / smart / angry)
2. Santa was first written about in America in __________. (280 AD / 1809 / 1822 / 1934 / 2018)
   a. The first jacket Santa Claus wore was __________. (red / yellow / blue / green)
   b. *The Night Before Christmas* told of a Santa who was __________. (fat / happy / short / All of these.)
3. Santa was never __________. (tall / married / named "Jeff" / small as an elf)
4. Later, Santa's jacket became __________ with a __________ fur trim. (blue, gold / white, red / gold, red / red, white)

Discussion:

I. Describe the best Christmas you have ever had.

The best Christmas I have ever had happened when I was __________ years old. I was in the city of ________________. The people with me were ______________________________. The weather was ________________. What we ate was ______________________________ ____________________, and what was so special about this time was ____________________ ____ ____.

II. Describe the places have you been to, or the trips you have made, during the Christmas holidays.

For Christmas I have been to ______________________________________. What I did there was ____. It (was / was not) fun because ____ ____.

III. What are some of the nicest presents you have ever received for Christmas or other special day? What are some of the nicest presents you have given to someone else?

The nicest present I have ever received was ______________________________.
To describe it, it was ____.
The nicest present I have given to someone else was ______________________.
To describe it, it was ____.

Word Fill: Complete the table with the given clues.

Year:	What Happened:	Other:
1. ________ AD	St. Nicholas was born	Where was this? ______________.
2. December 6	______________	How is the anniversary celebrated? ____________.
3. ________	______________	In what city was it written? ________________.
4. 1809	Sinter ________	His jacket was the color ________________.
5. ________	A Christmas poem	It was written by a ________________.
6. 1840	______________	Stores displayed pictures of ______________.
7. ________	In Philadelphia	People went to see the new ______________.
8. 1860s	______________	Showed Santa with a large white ________. He lived near the ____________ and elves made __________.
9. ________	Massachusetts	Some mall workers dressed as ____________ and his _______.
10. ________	______________	Asked the question ________________ Sometimes he was as tall as a ______________.
11. 1920	Santa's clothing	Wore a red suit, with ________________.
12. ________	Selling soft drink	Using Santa increased sales of ______________.
13. ________	The hit song	The name of the song is ________________.

Creative Thinking / Writing: *Be creative, and use your imagination!!*

1. Create two new things that will help Santa on his travels and explain what they do. (*Ex: Santa has a parrot that translates all the different languages and tells him which children are naughty and nice.*)
   Item I. ____.
   Item II. ____.

2. Create your own Santa character, and then draw the pictures suggested below.
   My own "Santa" is a ______________. Its name is ____________________.
   (He / She) wears a ______________________ that is ________________
   and has ______________________. The toys are made by ______________ in
   a very (small / large) ________________ that is located in the (country / city /
   ____________) that is called ________________. The presents are delivered
   on the date of ________________. This is because ________________.
   The presents are delivered to children by ______________________________.
   It will look like ________________________ and will go from city to city
   and house to house and powered by ______________________________.
   What I like most about this Santa character is that ______________________
   ____.

Here is a picture delivering presents. *Here is a happy child getting a gift.*

Opinion: Now tell the others about your Santa.

The person in my group who created the most interesting Santa is ____________. This is because ____.

Creative Storytelling: Now make up your own story about how your university came into being.

I. What animal started your university? (Ex: *a frog, turtle, fox, rabbit, etc.*). ______________.
I chose this animal because ______________________________.

II. Where is the animal from? What is its name? ______________________________.

III. What does the animal look like? (Ex: *The rabbit wore a red jacket with yellow sleeves, had long hair, and large round glasses*). ______________________________
______________________________.

IV. What special feature does the animal have? (Ex: *The rabbit had huge ears, which allowed it to listen and understand other people very carefully*). ______________________________
______________________________.

V. Why did the animal create your university? (Ex: *The rabbit needed to count carrots, so it created a university of math and computers*). ______________________________
______________________________.

VI. Additional Information: (Ex: *The rabbit was born in Aizu-Wakamatsu, but decided to leave there, so with its strong legs it hopped to Tokyo where it ...*). ______________________________
______________________________.

Creative Writing: Explain why and how your university was created.

*Our university was made ________ years ago by a ______________. The animal's name was ______________ and it came from ______________________________. It looks like ______________________________
______________________________. The special feature of the animal is that ______________________________. The animal decided to create my university because ______________________________
______________________________.*

In addition, ______________________________
______________________________.

Discussion / Presentation: Now tell the others your story. Ask lots of questions to clarify others' stories.

Opinion: *The person who told the most interesting story is ______________. This is because ______________________________.*

Debate: Is it ethical for parents to tell their child that Santa Claus exists? Why or why not?

Make up two questions of your own to discuss with the other class members. Be creative !!

6. The Same-Sex Wedding

Pre-Reading Question: When and where was the first same-sex wedding held in Japan?

Vocabulary: Match the words in bold with their meanings or descriptions.

1. certificate 証明書	2. civil partnership 市民パートナーシップ	3. gay 同性愛者
4. politician 政治家	5. slight majority 少しだけの多数派	6. symbolic 象徴的な
7. uncomfortable 居心地の悪い		

1. She was awarded a **certificate** for doing so well on the test.
2. The couple didn't receive a marriage certificate, but a **civil partnership**.
3. When he fell in love with a man, he knew he was **gay**.
4. One Japanese **politician** said something foolish, but later apologized.
5. A **slight majority** of people favored lowering the cost of education.
6. Today, the king has more **symbolic** significance.
7. When she gave her speech, Alice was not well prepared and felt very **uncomfortable**.

____ a. just more than half
____ b. to feel awkward
____ c. to have feelings for a person of the same sex
____ d. a kind of document
____ e. not an official marriage
____ f. to stand for something else
____ g. someone elected to a government position

7

[1] In March 2013, two women, Koyuki and her partner of one and a half years, Hiroko, got married at Tokyo Disney Resort. Koyuki first knew that she was **gay** as a high school student in Kanazawa. While working as an actress a couple of years later, she realized that "it was fine to be in love with another girl." The wedding ceremony itself was held in front of 30 of the couple's friends. The event made the news, so many more gay people throughout the country also celebrated. At the same time, Koyuki wrote, "My love Hiroko and I wore wedding dresses and had a mini-parade at Disney Sea, a place I also love," then continued, "I was really happy!" Koyuki then wrote on Twitter, "My partner Hiroko and I just had a gay wedding at the Tokyo Disney Resort. Even Mickey and Minnie are here to celebrate with us." One newspaper headline said, "Mickey Mouse supports gay marriage!"

[2] Disney had been allowing same-sex weddings to be held in their U.S. and other parks since 2007, but this was the first such wedding to take place in Japan. At first, Disney said that the two women had to dress "like a man and a woman" so that other park visitors would not feel **uncomfortable**. But within a week, Disney apologized, and the couple were told that they could dress in any way they wanted. Disney wrote, "If we caused them sadness and discomfort, we are sorry."

[3] While the wedding itself was not legally recognized in Japan, there are no laws against being gay, and there is little if anything opposed to homosexuality in Buddhism and Shinto. Hiroko said, "Mostly, we just wanted people to know that gay people exist for real, and that we would like to have weddings just like everyone else." Hence, while the wedding was only **symbolic**, it was perhaps the first step towards helping to create a dialog about same-sex marriage. Japan's gay community is growing and homosexuality is becoming more common. Taiga Ishikawa, a gay **politician**, said, "This is only a guess, but I'd say there are more gay people now who are in long-term relationships and want them to at least be recognized in the form of a **civil partnership**."

[4] In 2013, a poll found that a **slight majority** of Japanese people support making same-sex partnerships or marriages legal. In 2015 in Shibuya in Tokyo, Koyuki and Hiroko received a certificate that recognizes their same-sex civil partnership. This was a first in Japan. Although it is not an official marriage **certificate**, it is considered to be another step towards marriage equality. With her wife by her side, Koyuki said, "I'm so happy ... when they gave us the certificate, I cried. Our friends cried, too."

"I love Mickey Mouse more than any woman I have ever known."

– Walt Disney

Active Outline: Choose the correct answer.

1. Two women got married in Disneyland after going out for __________ years. (1.5 / 2.5 / 5)
   a. The wedding was held in front of __________ friends. (twenty / thirty / fifty)
   b. The mini-parade was held at __________. (Disney Sea / Disney California / Kanazawa / Shibuya)
2. This was the first same-sex wedding to take place at Tokyo Disneyland __________.
   (since 2007 / with 30 friends / with a mini-parade / ever)
3. The marriage is legally recognized throughout Japan. (True / False)
   a. The gay community in Japan is becoming __________. (larger / smaller)
4. In 2013, __________ Japanese supported either the civil partnership or marriage of same-sex couples. (few / a slight majority of / most / all)
   a. Two years later, the couple received a certificate in __________ that recognizes their union. (Ginza / Shibuya / Tokyo / Japan / the world)
   b. After receiving the certificate, the couple cried because they were so __________.
   (happy / sad / tired / angry / hungry)

Critical Thinking:

What are reasons for and against making gay marriage legal in Japan?

For gay marriage:	Against gay marriage:
1. ______________________________	1. ______________________________
2. ______________________________	2. ______________________________

Opinion: If you had been at Tokyo Disneyland on the day of Koyuki and Hiroko's wedding, and were invited to attend it, would you have done so? Why or why not?

Writing / Discussion: Answer and then discuss the questions with your classmates.

I. Many universities in America have "gay" clubs and circles for people who are interested in the lifestyle and who want to support one another. Should there be a gay club at your school? Why or why not?

Opinion: When do you think there will be a gay club at your school? If you don't think there will ever be one, explain why not.

II. Assume that you have a relative who recently "came out" as gay. What would your reaction be towards him/her? Explain.

Opinion: Would you attend the wedding of your gay relative? Why or why not?

Sentence Unscramble and Sequence Order: Put the words in order to make complete sentences. Then put the events in the order that they happened. Label the first event "A," the second "B," and so on.

1. ____ met / Koyuki / another woman, / they decided / married. / and / to get

   ____

2. A gay. / In / was / Koyuki knew / high school, / that she

   ____

3. ____ certificate / they were / their / In Shibuya, / partnership. / given a / that recognizes

   ____

4. ____ wedding / The / Disneyland. / was held / Tokyo / at / ceremony

   ____

5. ____ Mickey Mouse / wrote / that / marriage. / A newspaper / gay / supports

   ____

6. ____ to / realized / Koyuki / be / it's OK / gay. / that

   ____

7. D Disney / to dress / apologized. / said the couple / had / but after / as a / and female, / male

   ____

Creative Writing: Write a "report" of a gay wedding that you might have attended. Be creative, and use your imagination!!

A few years ago, I learned that my ______________ was gay. At the time, I (did / did not) understand it. However, I eventually realized that ______________________________ ______________________________. About _______ months ago, I was told that (he / she) would soon be getting married, and that I was invited. I decided to go because ____.

I went to the city of ______________________________, which is where the wedding took place. It was a beautiful place, with lots of fresh air and ______________________. What I liked most about this place was that ______________________________. The weather was especially ____________ and you could smell ______________________.

About ____________ people attended the wedding, and when the couple kissed, I felt ____. The wedding cake was ____________ and had the flavor of ____________. It was ____________________. After the celebration, we went to __________________, where there was a big party. What I liked most about the party ____ ______________. Overall, the event was __________________, and what I learned was that ____.

My Feedback: Give feedback and write down some questions to ask the speakers.

______________________________ ______________________________

______________________________ ______________________________

Creative Story: Pretend that a few weeks ago, you attended a gay wedding. Write a paragraph in which you "report" about the experience. Use the paragraph above as a model.

Debate: Write down and then discuss these questions with your classmates.

I. Do you think that life is difficult for gay people in Japan? Why or why not? Be specific.

II. Should the laws be changed to allow gay marriage in Japan? Why or why not?

Make up two questions of your own to discuss with the other class members. Be creative !!

7. World Festivals

Pre-Reading Question: Describe a festival from somewhere in the world that you know of.

Vocabulary: Match the words with their meanings or descriptions.

1. afterlife 死後の生活	2. bullfighting 闘牛	3. bulls 雄牛
4. haunted house お化け屋敷	5. Lent 四旬節（レント）	6. leprechauns レプラカーン（伝説の妖精）
7. pinch 傷つける	8. skeletons 骸骨	9. souls 魂

____ a. people's spirits
____ b. the bones in the body
____ c. life after death
____ d. with two fingers, gently squeeze
____ e. a Christian holiday
____ f. a scary building
____ g. a man versus bull
____ h. large animals with horns
____ i. small green creatures

Vocabulary: Fill in the blanks in the questions and answers below with the correct words.

A. **Question**: What can I find inside the ______? **Answer**: There are lots of ______ and scary ghosts.

B. **Question**: What happens in the ______?
Answer: Many believe that after death, people's ______ travel to another world.

C. **Question**: On St. Patrick's Day, what do small, green ______ do to people who aren't wearing green?
Answer: They ______ them on the arm.

D. **Question**: Where did you go for the ______ holidays?
Answer: We went to a large stadium and watched the men and the ______ doing the ______.

CD 8

"The real voyage of discovery is not in seeking new places,
but in seeing with new eyes." – ***Marcel Proust***

[1] Many fascinating festivals are held all over the world all the year round. Perhaps you can plan your next vacation around one of these celebrations.

[2] Brazil: *Carnival*. Carnival is held in early February and lasts four days. Carnival, which began in 1928, is perhaps the best-known and most exciting festival in the world. Over two million people take part, and the whole country stops for nearly a week of celebrations. Carnival marks the beginning of the Catholic holiday of **Lent**. Rio de Janeiro is the site of the largest Carnival, although many smaller ones are put on across the country for anyone to attend. Overall, Carnival is an exciting parade of energetic dancing, vibrant colors, lots of alcohol, and costumes of all kinds – with some people wearing almost nothing at all!

[3] Munich, Germany: *Oktoberfest*. This festival began way back in 1810. It is a yearly event that lasts about 16 days – from the end of September through early October. Called the world's largest beer festival, it features live music, parades, performers, game booths, roller coasters, **haunted houses**, and lots of great German food. But the most important attraction is beer, with many large tents selling every kind of beer for about 9 euros or around 1,100 yen.

[4] Ireland: *St. Patrick's Day*. The festival is held on March 17 and celebrates Saint Patrick of Ireland. But what it really celebrates is being Irish – or, perhaps, just wishing to be Irish. Until the 1970s, it was a religious holiday. The first St. Patrick's Day parade was held in New York City in 1762; it is now the largest St. Patrick's Day parade in the world. In Dublin and throughout Ireland, the festival lasts for a week. People are supposed to wear something green during that time, because, according to legend, **leprechauns** would **pinch** anyone not wearing that color. During the daytime, Dublin offers different walking tours throughout the city, and in the evening, many famous buildings are lit up in green, which is called the "Greening the City." Many younger people paint their face green, the country comes alive with dancing, concerts, fireworks, outdoor theater, lots of drinking, live music, and even a 5k run.

[5] Mexico: *Day of the Dead*. The origins of this festival, which lasts from October 31 to November 2, go back hundreds of years. It celebrates and remembers loved ones who have died and perhaps need support to move to the **afterlife**. Favorite items, candies, and other gifts are brought to the children and relatives of those who have died – and lots of flowers, too, which are thought to attract the **souls** of the dead. Pillows and blankets are left out along with candles, pictures of relatives, and religious statues are left at grave sites so the dead can rest on their long journey. Many people dress up in scary costumes such as **skeletons** and ghosts to celebrate the day, along with dancing, art, parades, picnics, street parties, and prayer sessions. Though it sounds sad, it is a colorful, joyful holiday that does not fear death, but celebrates the life beyond this one.

[6] Spain: *The Running of the **Bulls***. The festival is a combination of **bullfighting** and religion. It is held early in July and offers a one-of-a-kind experience. Scores of bulls chase after people, who run 825 meters through the city streets. As the bulls are let out into the street, the runners sprint as quickly as they can to avoid them. Running in front of angry bulls doesn't sound like fun, but many people love it. Runners must be physically fit, and they all accept that this is a dangerous race. This huge party features fireworks, music, and bullfighting, and attracts thousands of tourists. Of course, most people just watch and take pictures at a safe distance.

"Twenty years from now, you will be more disappointed by the things you didn't do than by the ones you did do." – ***Mark Twain***

Active Outline: Choose the correct answer.

1. There are many festivals around the world that are interesting and well worth seeing. (True / False)
2. Perhaps the most famous festival is _________.
   (Carnival / Oktoberfest / Day of the Dead / St. Patrick's Day).
   a. Carnival is only held in Brazil's biggest city, Rio de Janeiro. (True / False)
3. Oktoberfest is the world's largest _________ festival. (live music / flower / parade / beer)
   a. There are no _________ at Oktoberfest.
   (game booths / haunted houses / performers / graves)
4. The largest St. Patrick's Day parade is held in _________. (Ireland / New York / London / Tokyo)
   a. On St. Patrick's Day, people are supposed to wear the color _________.
   (red / orange / blue / green)
5. Mexico's Day of the Dead festival celebrates _________.
   (praying / candy / people who have died / picnics)
   a. People wear all of these costumes except _________. (animals / skeletons / ghosts)
   b. The festival is overall a _________ one. (depressing / gloomy / fun / new)

6. At the Running of the Bulls, people run __________ the bulls. (in front of / behind / towards / to find)
   a. The race __________ dangerous. (could be / is never)
   b. Most people __________ the bulls. (run with / take pictures of)

Comprehension: Which of these festivals would you most like to go to? Rank them in order from most (1) to least (5).

___ Carnival ___ Oktoberfest ___ St. Patrick's Day
___ Day of the Dead ___ The Running of the Bulls

Opinion: Which of these festivals would you most like to go to? Why?

The festival I would most like to attend is _______________. This is because _______________
____.

Opinion: Which of these festivals do you consider the strangest? Would you or would you not like to attend it? Explain.

The festival I consider the strangest is _____________. I (would / would not) like to go to it because ____
____.

Matching: Match the festivals with their descriptions. (There is one extra answer.)

1. **Carnival** ___ A. Parade, wearing green, drinking, singing
2. **Oktoberfest** ___ B. Drinking green beer, dressing up as ghosts, running from bulls
3. **St. Patrick's Day** ___ C. Bullfighting, danger, religion, city streets
4. **Day of the Dead** ___ D. Nonstop parade, dancing, colorful costumes, Lent
5. **The Running of the Bulls** ___ E. Honor the dead, picnics, praying, scary costumes
___ F. Beer, live music, performers, game booths, German food

Creative Writing / Presentation: Tell your classmates about a festival that you recently attended. Also, don't forget to draw "photos" in the spaces provide. Be Creative. Be interesting!!

I went to a festival recently that celebrates _______________________. It's located in _______________. Since it's in the _______________ season, the weather was _______________. I went with three people, including _____________, _____________, and _____________. The festival itself (was / was not) crowded. There was a large parade with many people marching in it. The most memorable costumes were people dressed _______________________________. Many people wore _______________________________ in the colors ___________ and ___________ with a large ___________. I thought it was _______________________. What I found most interesting about the parade was _______________________ _______________________. On one side of the festival there was a band playing, and I saw that there were _______________________. Overall, their music was _______________________. One of the band members _______________________. On the other side there were people selling food, and I had some _______________, and some _______________ for dessert. The festival lasted until _______________, and we then all decided to _______________________________.

Here are some photos that I took.

This picture is ________ ________

Here we saw ________ ________

This is a ________ ________

My Feedback: Give feedback and write down some questions to ask the speakers.

________ ________

________ ________

Creative Storytelling: Create your own festival. Be creative, and use your imagination!!

I. What is the name of the festival? (Ex: *The name of this festival is Spot, because we are celebrating my beautiful dog.)* ________.

II. What does it celebrate? *For this festival, we celebrate* ________ ________.

III. Where is it held? *This festival is held in* ________.

IV. When did this festival first begin? *This festival began back in the year* ________.

V. When does it take place each year?
The festival will take place ________ *and I chose this day because* ________.

VI. What is / are the festival's most important (color / colors)?
The festival's most important color(s) (is / are) ________, *and this is because* ________.

VII. About how many people will attend this festival?
I hope that ________ *people will attend this festival.*

VIII. What are at least three items or activities that this festival is known for?
The biggest and most important (item / event) of the festival is the ________.
There will also be ________ *and* ________.

Writing: Now describe the festival in a short essay. What happens? Give lots of details!

____

____

________.

My Feedback: Write down some questions to ask the speakers.

________? ________?

________? ________?

Make up two questions of your own to discuss with the other class members. Be creative !!

8. What Makes You Happier: Experiences or Luxury Goods?

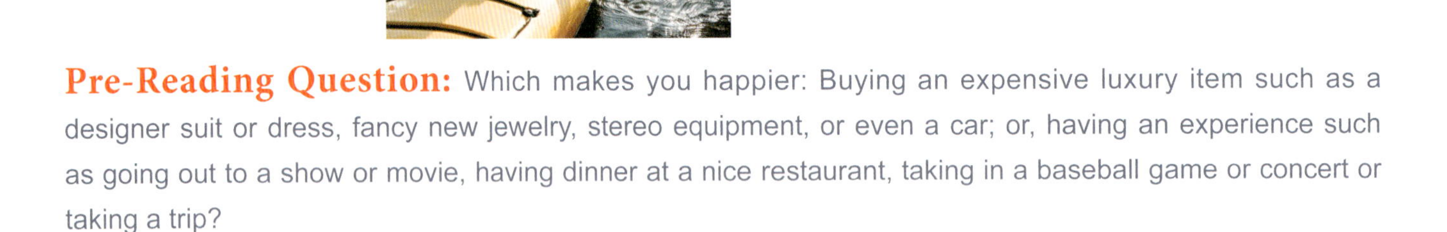

Pre-Reading Question: Which makes you happier: Buying an expensive luxury item such as a designer suit or dress, fancy new jewelry, stereo equipment, or even a car; or, having an experience such as going out to a show or movie, having dinner at a nice restaurant, taking in a baseball game or concert or taking a trip?

Vocabulary: Match the words with their meanings or descriptions.

1. basic needs are met 基本的欲求が満たされる
2. envy ねたみ
3. fade 徐々に消える
4. frustrated いらいらする
5. remodeling 改築
6. souvenirs 土産

____ a. to be upset or angry
____ b. small gifts, usually brought home from travel
____ c. to improving a building
____ d. the minimum needed, such as food and shelter
____ e. to resent or become jealous
____ f. to weaken or becomes less

Vocabulary: Fill in the blanks in the sentences below with the correct word.

A. They felt ______ after their neighbors had done some extensive ______ to their home.
B. Once our ______, we can get nicer, more expensive things.
C. Bob was ______ because the colors of his favorite Hawaiian shirt had begun to ______.
D. When we traveled to Aizu-Wakamatsu, we bought lots of ______.

CD 9

"Wealth is the ability to fully experience life."
– Henry David Thoreau

[1] Most of us think that we will be happier for a longer time after we buy an expensive luxury item rather than after having some sort of experience. After all, luxury items such as a Gucci wallet, a Louis Vuitton bag, designer clothes, expensive accessories, state-of-the-art stereo equipment, gold jewelry, the latest iPhone, a large TV, a flashy car, or **remodeling** your home certainly lasts longer than a trip, say, which eventually gives way to only memories, with perhaps a few photographs and **souvenirs** to remind us of it. However, research on what makes people happier has found the opposite to be true; we get far greater pleasure from having an experience than from buying "stuff." After our **basic needs are met**, many of us think that buying fancy items or filling our house with lots of expensive items will make us extremely happy. It is true that when we buy something new, we become happy – for a short time. Unfortunately, after a few months, that expensive, "cool" new item will no longer make us happy. Its pleasures will soon **fade**, get "old," and we will want something else that is newer, larger, nicer.

[2] Experiences can be something as simple as going to a coffee shop or taking in movies, plays, concerts, ball games, or art shows. Experiences also include activities such as hiking, exercising, singing, dancing, and playing sports. Learning to paint or speak another language, practicing yoga, cooking, or playing a musical instrument also offer great experiences and usually allow us to socialize – to meet and talk with other people.

[3] As time goes on, our happiness with a new item decreases. But with time, our happiness with experiences increases. Even difficult, bad experiences will often change into happy memories or funny stories. For example, if you had a hard time in school, in a few years, you will remember it in a way that will seem better than it actually was, and you may look back on it with warmth and humor.

[4] Two people are more likely to create a friendship during experiences such as climbing Mt. Fuji or visiting a park together than by owning a similar car, clothes, or other items. They are more likely to enjoy each other's company when they are discussing experiences than when comparing "stuff" they own, which can even leave them **frustrated**. For example, you can't really compare a walk in the park with a yoga class. But you can compare things we have bought, which can lead to **envy** and resentment.

[5] Thus, if you want to be happier, accumulate experiences instead of fancy items. Experiences create a bigger "us" than do the items we own. Experiences not only make us happier, but they also last forever. Experiences bring us closer to others, eventually giving us a stronger sense of self and becoming a part of our identity.

"We make a living by what we get, but we make a life by what we give."
– Winston Churchill

Active Outline: Choose the correct answer.

1. Most people assume that they will be happier after _________ something. (buying / experiencing)
   a. Most people think that buying the newest and most expensive thing _________ make them happy. (will / will not)
   b. Often, within a few _________, that cool new item you bought will feel old and dated. (days / weeks / months / years)
2. Experiences can include _________. (going to the ballet / playing tennis / a trip to Aizu-Wakamatsu / All of these. / None of these.)
3. In time, our happiness with items _________, while our happiness with experiences _________. (decreases, decreases / increases, increases / increases, decreases / decreases, increases)
4. Two people are more likely to "connect" because they have shared the same _________. (experience / item)
5. It is _________ that become part of your identity. (those things you own/ your experiences)

Critical / Creative Thinking: List five expensive items that you own and five experiences that you have had.

Luxury Items you own. (Ex: *a nice wallet*). **Experiences** you have had. (Ex: *playing ping pong*).

1. ____________________ ____________________
2. ____________________ ____________________
3. ____________________ ____________________
4. ____________________ ____________________
5. ____________________ ____________________

Opinion: With a partner, discuss some of the items and experiences you wrote above. On a scale of 1 to 10, ten being highest, what was your level of happiness for each?

*While rating **items**, on a scale of 1 to 10 I felt a ______. This is because ______________________________.*

*While rating **experiences**, on a scale of 1 to 10 I felt a ______. This is because ______________________________.*

Writing / Discussion Exercise:

I. Write about a time over a year ago when you got some expensive item (such as a nice watch, clothes, name-brand bag or wallet, jewelry, etc.) Describe the item, where you got it, and how you felt when you bought it.

About _____ year(s) ago, I bought a really nice __________. I got it in __________, and I bought it because ______________________. After I bought it, I felt ______________, because ______________________.

Opinion: How happy does the item make you feel now (scale of 1 to 10).

When looking back at the item, on a scale from 1 to 10, I now feel a _____. This is because ______________________.

II. Write about a time over a year ago when you had an experience (such as visited relatives, went to a concert, played volleyball, etc.) Describe the experience you had, where it took place, and how you felt about it at the time.

About _____ year(s) ago, I went to ______________________. What happened was ______________________.

At the time, the experience was ______________________.

As it happened, I felt ______________________,

because ______________________.

Opinion: How happy does the experience make you feel now (scale of 1 to 10).

When looking back at the experience, on a scale from 1 to 10, I now feel a _____. This is because ______________________.

Discussion:

With a partner, discuss which you now rank higher, the expensive item or the experience you had.

The (expensive item / experience) has the higher ranking and has made me happier. This is because ______________________________
For example, I ______________________________
______________________________.

Matching:
Based on today's reading, match the sentence beginnings and endings.

1. It was found that people are happier when they ___ A. having a cup of coffee together.
2. When we buy an expensive item, we ___ B. have an experience.
3. That expensive item we just bought soon ___ C. become part of our identity.
4. Experiences can be as simple as ___ D. expensive items as luxury watches.
5. Even bad experiences will ___ E. becomes dated and its pleasure fades.
6. We may get envious when we compare ___ F. become very happy for a short time.
7. Memories bring us closer to other people and ___ G. become better in time.

Presentation / Discussion:

Think of a special time or experience you have had. Which is more important to you now, your memories of the experience, or the things you still have that are related to the experience? If it were possible to choose, would you rather keep your memories of the experience or the things associated with it?

A special time that I had was ______________. *It happened* ______________ *(months / years) ago. What happened was* ______________________________
______________. *What was most special to me about that day was* ______________________________.

If I had to choose between keeping all my memories from that day, or keeping everything linked to that day, including the things I wore, all the presents I bought, pictures I took, etc., I would keep (the memories / everything associated with the experience). This is because ______________________________
______________________________.

Debate:
Overall, do you agree with the ideas expressed in today's reading? Will they change your behavior? If yes, how? If no, why not? Discuss this question with your classmates.

Make up two questions of your own to discuss with the other class members. Be creative !!

9. Teenagers and Stress

Pre-Reading Question: Who do you think has more stress, teenagers or adults?

Vocabulary: Match the sentence beginnings with their endings.

1. fitting in 溶け込む	2. manage 制御する	3. miserable 惨めな
4. motivate 動機付ける	5. nap 昼寝	6. pressure プレッシャー
7. procrastinating 先延ばしにすること	8. teased いじめられる	

1. The new kids had difficulty **fitting in**, but wanted
2. It is important to **manage** and
3. A small amount of stress can **motivate**
4. They were **miserable**
5. Sometimes, I will take a **nap**
6. Students have a lot of **pressure**
7. She was **procrastinating**
8. One student was **teased** and

____ a. that can lead to high levels of stress.
____ b. made fun of for being “different.”
____ c. and putting off studying for the exam.
____ d. to be like everyone else.
____ e. people to do things.
____ f. when they lost the game.
____ g. control your stress levels.
____ h. or a short rest in the afternoon.

10

[1] Teenagers very often feel lots of stress. Of course, their stress levels are usually higher during the school year and lower during the vacations. Studies have found that when a person starts to feel stress at an early age, it often continues into later life. Many teens expect their stress levels to increase in the future. Today's teenagers have a higher level of stress overall compared to their parents. This comes from the **pressure** that teens feel resulting from the demands of social life, school, work, and other activities. Among the biggest worries that teenagers have are not **fitting in**; not having friends; being judged or **teased**; failing in school; and not being attractive enough.

[2] A little stress can be a good thing, because it can **motivate** us to plan ahead and get our work done. But for many teenagers, too much stress is linked to headaches, poor sleep, anger, sadness, depression, fatigue, or trouble with classmates. Often, while under stress, teenagers will eat unhealthy foods or overeat, or, on the other hand, skip meals altogether. Many do not get enough sleep or exercise. When their stress becomes too difficult to handle, they may even become **miserable**.

[3] It is important that you **manage** your stress wisely and carefully. To do this, you can, for example, take a short break every so often to reward yourself and to do things that you enjoy doing and that makes you feel good, whether it is baking or cooking something delicious, studying yoga, or listening to your favorite music.

It is also very important to make time for socializing with friends and simply having fun. Many teenagers play sports or exercise once or twice a week for at least 30 minutes. That's a great stress reliever. So take a long walk, go for a run, or go for a ride on your bike. Exercise cheers you up and makes you feel better and more motivated. Eat healthy food. Get seven to eight hours of sleep a night and take a daytime **nap**. Keep yourself organized. Clean your room and tidy your closet. If the place where you work is cluttered, "fix" it by throwing out what you don't need.

[4] And most of all, limit the amount of time you devote to unhealthy activities such as playing video games or spending hours online. Limit such things as watching TV to a reasonable amount of time, say 30 minutes at a time. These things waste a lot of time and actually add to your stress. If you have too much work to do, write all the things you have to do down and try to calculate how long each item will take to complete. When we write things down, we can often plan ahead, which keeps us from **procrastinating**. We naturally feel great pleasure as we cross each item off our list.

[5] Another important stress "buster" is to always choose friends who support what you are doing. Do not complain to everyone about how stressed you are. Complaining about your stress levels only makes it worse. In addition, it can upset and even "turn off" your friends and family. And if you think you need help to deal with your stress, get it from a qualified professional.

Up in the morning and out to school.
The teacher is teaching the golden rule.
American history and practical math.
You studying hard and hoping to pass.
Working your fingers right down to the bone.
And the guy behind you won't leave you alone.

– Chuck Berry, School Days

Active Outline: Choose the correct answer.

1. Teenagers have higher stress during holidays. (True / False)
   a. Studies have found that teenagers have a ________ level of stress than adults. (higher / lower)
2. Even a small amount of stress is bad. (True / False)
   a. While under stress, teenagers often do not get enough ________. (food / sleep / exercise / All of these.)
3. It ________ important that we manage our stress level. (is / is not)
   a. Exercise can help improve your mood. (True / False)
4. One thing you can do to manage your stress is to ________. (watch TV / write things down / sleep less than seven hours a night / skip meals)
5. You ________ complain to your friends and family about your stress. (should / should not)

Creative Writing: Write about a real or imaginary friend. Make sure you include three pieces of good "stress-busting" advice at the end.

I have a very good friend named ____________, and I noticed that recently (he / she) has had a lot of stress. (He / She) says that there's a lot of stress from school. But what causes my friend the most stress is ________________________________. All of this stress is affecting my friend a lot because ________________________ ________________________. Also, (he / she) is not (doing) ____________

________________________________. My friend and I discussed the problem. I believe that the biggest problem is ____.

I gave my friend three pieces of advice that I hope will help with the problem. Here is what I said.

1. ________________________________
2. ________________________________
3. ________________________________

My Feedback: Give feedback and write down some questions to ask the speakers.

____________________? ____________________?

____________________? ____________________?

Critical Thinking:

1. What two items listed in today's reading do you do or don't do?

Do:	Don't Do:
1. ____________	1. ____________
2. ____________	2. ____________

Opinion: What advice would you add to the reading that would help people manage their stress?

The advice I would add to the article to help people manage their stress would be to ____.

This should help by ________________________________.

2. What three items in the reading did you find most helpful?

____________ ____________ ____________

Opinion: What was the most helpful piece of advice in the reading?

The most helpful piece of advice I found in the reading was that I should ________________________ It would help me (because / by) ____.

Matching: Based on today's reading, match the sentence beginnings and endings.

1. Teenagers have a lot of stress and	____	A. school work, social life, and other activities.
2. Teens feel pressures from	____	B. a break and make time for friends and fun.
3. Some stress is a good thing because	____	C. playing video games or watching TV.
4. To manage stress, you should take	____	D. clean your room and toss your old things away.
5. To stay better organized, you should	____	E. they expect it to get worse in the future.
6. You should not spend too much time	____	F. it motivates you to get things done.

Writing:

1. Do you feel you have a lot of stress?

   I (do / do not) feel that I have a lot of stress. This is because ______________________________

   ____.

2. In the future, do you think your stress level will increase or decrease? Why?

   In the future, I think that my stress level will (increase / decrease). This is because ______

   ____.

3. Have your stress levels gotten lower or higher in the past few years?

   I feel that my stress levels have gotten (lower / higher) in the past few years. This is because ____.

4. How do you manage your stress?

   What I do to manage my stress is ______________________________________.

   For example, ____.

   In addition I also ____

   ____.

Discussion:

Speak to a partner. What is his or her greatest source of stress?

(He / She) said that the greatest source of stress is ______________________________

____.

Opinion: What advice would you give your partner to help him or her manage stress?

The advice from the reading that I would give my partner is ______________________

____.

My own advice that I would give my partner is ______________________________

____.

Debate: Write down and then discuss this question with your classmates.

What can Japan do as a society to help reduce its level of stress?

What Japan can do to help limit people's stress is to ______________________________

____.

This is because ____

____

____.

Make up two questions of your own to discuss with the other class members. Be creative !!

10. Superheroes

Pre-Reading Question: What superheroes do you know and like? How did they begin? Describe them.

Vocabulary: Fill in the blanks in the sentences below with the correct word.

1. accident-prone nerd 事故を起こしやすいオタク		2. awkward 不器用な
3. bullied いじめた	4. clay 粘土	5. craze 流行
6. golden lasso 金の投げ縄	7. x-ray vision X 線視覚（透視能力）	

A. Hello Kitty began the ______ for cute things.
B. She claimed to see through walls using ______.
C. It was made of soft ______.
D. The rope painted yellow was actually a ______.
E. He was an ______ who was at times really ______, for which he was ______.

CD 11

"I think people have always loved things that are bigger than life, things that are imaginative."

– Stan Lee

[1] Superman was created in 1933 by two high school students living in the U.S. state of Ohio. Superman became a comic book in 1938 and began the **craze** for adventure-seeking superheroes dressed in unique costumes. Superman was born with the name Kal-El on the planet Krypton. Before the planet exploded, his father put the child in a rocket that landed on Earth, in rural America. He was taken in by the Kent's, a couple who owned a farm. They named him Clark and brought him up with strong morals. He was taught to hide his identity as Superman and to use his superpowers only for good. As a young adult, Clark moved to the city of Metropolis and wrote for a newspaper, *The Daily Planet*. Clark fell in love with Lois Lane, who rejected "Clark" but fell in love with "Superman." He used his powers to protect his family, friends, and others – and the Earth itself – from bad people. Superman's costume was blue and red, with a red cape. His superpowers included heat vision, flight, super-speed movement, super hearing, and many others. He could be weakened by coming into contact with kryptonite, and while lead was the only substance that could block kryptonite's bad effects, Superman could not see through lead using his **x-ray vision**. His powers would also weaken if he was not able to go near the sun for a long time.

[2] By the 1940s, other superheroes had come into being, including Batman and the Green Lantern. And for the first time ever, a female superhero appeared with her own series: Wonder Woman. The goal was to create a female superhero with the strength of Superman who is at the same time wise and beautiful, a role model for females as both woman and superhero. Wonder Woman often defeated evil without a fight, using kindness, compassion, and love – but never appearing weak. She is now probably the most recognizable female superhero. Diana – Wonder Woman's name – was born in 3,000 BC on Paradise Island, an island of great female warriors called the Amazons. Her mother had created her out of **clay**, and the Greek gods gave her life and her amazing superpowers. Growing up, she was trained as a fighter. When Steve Trevor's airplane crashes on Paradise Island in 1941, Diana finds him, brings him back to health, and falls in love with him. Since men are not allowed on the island, Steve must return to America. The Queen of the Amazons has a contest to decide who will return Steve to "man's world." Diana wins; but as Wonder Woman, she must represent Paradise Island and fight against evil. She can run as fast as 97 km/h and, for protection, uses a **golden lasso** that makes people tell the truth. She also has a crown that turns into a weapon when thrown into the air and bracelets for protection. Sometimes she uses other items like a magic sword and an invisible airplane that can fly into space.

[3] Spider-Man, introduced in 1962, was a new and different type of superhero. Unlike the others, who are older, wise, and powerfully built, Spider-Man is young and immature, with a slim, boyish look. While brilliant in science, Peter Parker (Spider-Man's human name) is an **awkward** teenager with poor social skills. He is an **accident-prone nerd** who is often **bullied**, scared of girls, and even has money problems. While he always tries to do the right thing, he still questions whether he is helpful. College students soon identified with Spider-Man, and he quickly became their favorite superhero. In the Spider-Man story, Peter Parker's parents died in an airplane crash, so his Uncle Ben and Aunt May raised him in New York City. In high school, he went to a science exhibit, where he was bitten by a radioactive spider. This bite gave him his superpowers, including super-quickness, amazing strength, and the ability to sense danger ahead using his "spider-senses." He could climb walls and ceilings and could shoot webs from his wrists. He soon learned that "with great power, comes great responsibility." To help his aunt with her finances, he gets a job at a newspaper, *The Daily Bugle*, and sells pictures of himself as Spider-Man. The publisher, J. Jonah Jameson, uses the newspaper to call Spider-Man a criminal, and unlike other superheroes, Spider-Man is not always liked or trusted by the public, who often think of him as an outlaw.

"Imagination is more important than knowledge. Knowledge is limited. Imagination encircles the world."

– Albert Einstein

Active Outline: Choose the correct answer.

1. Superman was written by __________ students. (high school / college / working / all of these)
   a. He was born with the name __________. (Kal-El / Clark Kent / Lois Lane / Lex Luthor)
   b. In the city, he worked for a __________. (farm / bookstore / newspaper / advertising agency)
   c. Lead protects him from __________. (Lois Lane / the sun / kryptonite / None of these.)
2. Wonder Woman is a model for __________. (superheroes / men / women / children)
   a. She was born __________. (in Japan / in America / on Paradise Island / in space)
3. Spider-Man is __________ mature than other superheroes. (more / less)
   a. J. Jonah Jameson __________ like Spider-Man. (does / does not)

Word Fill: Read the descriptions. Write **SU** for Superman, **WW** for Wonder Woman, or **SM** for Spider-Man.

1. Uses kindness and compassion ___	Is from a small island ___	Has a red cape ___
2. Can fly to space in an airplane ___	Liked by college students ___	Good at science ___
3. Is wise and beautiful ___	Not trusted by people ___	Has x-ray vision ___
4. The first to wear a costume ___	Is from another planet ___	A nerd ___
5. Works for *The Daily Planet* ___	Can feel danger ahead ___	Climbs walls ___
6. Is in high school ___	Brought up on a farm ___	Lives in New York ___
7. Was trained in fighting ___	Has heat vision ___	Is afraid of girls ___

Opinion: Which one of these characters do you like the most? What makes him/her so interesting? Why?

The character I like the most is _______. The thing I like most about (him / her) is _______ _______________. This is because _______________.

Writing: Who is your favorite superhero character? How did he/she come into being? What makes him/her interesting?

My very favorite superhero character is ______________. (His / Her) background is ____.

The most interesting thing about this character is that ____.

Group Discussion: In your group, talk about one another's very favorite superhero characters.

Notes: ____.

Creative Storytelling: Create a superhero character of your own. *Be Creative. Be interesting!!*

I. **Basics**: What is your character's name? Is it male or female?

The character's name is ______________. It is (male / female). The character is a ______________ and looks like ______________________________. The character's weight and height are ______________________.

II. **Background story**: What is your character's background story? (Ex: Batman saw his parents killed. The Hulk was a scientist). A good story allows people to better understand and relate to the character.

My character is from ______________ and this place is a (city / state / countryside / ______________). It (is / is not) a real place. The character began by ______________________________. He / she first notices the ability to ______________________________. When the character first finds out of this, (he / she) is (glad / unhappy) because ______________________________. The community (likes / dislikes) the character, because ______________. As the character grows, their abilities change by ______________________.

III. **Attitude**: What happened in the past that made your character want to fight evil or to become what he/she is?

The reason why my character fights evil is that ______________________________.

IV. **Personality**: What kind of person is your character? Don't give all positive or all negative ratings. A complex, imperfect character is more interesting!

Positive				Negative	Positive				Negative
Nice	*	*	*	Mean	Caring	*	*	*	Uncaring
Smart	*	*	*	Stupid	Aggressive	*	*	*	Lazy
Outgoing	*	*	*	Shy	Honest	*	*	*	Dishonest

Discussion Activity: Get feedback on the character you have created so far from the others in your group.

The feedback I got from the others is ____________________ . What they like about my character is ____________________ . They suggested that I could improve my character by ____________________ .

V. **Powers**: Every superhero has superpowers (ability to fly), skills (excellent swimmer), or something to help (protection bracelets). What superpowers, skills, and/or items does your superhero have?

1. ____________________ 2. ____________________
3. ____________________ 4. ____________________
5. ____________________ 6. ____________________

VI. **Weakness**: It is the weakness of the character that makes him or her so interesting. What is your character's weakness?

1. ____________________ 2. ____________________

VII. **Creative Drawing**: Superman's costume has a yellow shield with a red "S" on the chest. Spider-Man has a spider. What does your character's costume look like? What are the costume's colors? What appears on your character's chest? Draw your images here.

This is what the character looks like. This is on the character's chest.

Opinion: What is your character's most outstanding feature?

VIII. **Creative Saying**: Superman is known as "*The Man of Steel*." Wonder Woman is called "*The Goddess of Love and War*." Spider-Man's nicknames are "*Webhead*" and "*Wall-Crawler*." He also has the quote, "*With great power comes great responsibility*." Make up a short, memorable nickname or quote for your character.

The (nickname / quote) that goes with my character is ____________________ .
The reason I chose this (nickname / quote) is ____________________ .

Discussion Activity: Get feedback on your character from the others in your group.

The feedback I got from the others is ____________________ . What they like about my character is ____________________ .

They suggested that I should improve my character by ____________________ .

Make up two questions of your own to discuss with the other class members. Be creative !!

11. Gratitude

Pre-Reading Question: Does being happy make you more grateful, or does being grateful make you happier?

Vocabulary: Fill in the blanks in the sentences below with the correct word.

1. appreciate 感謝する	2. depression 落ち込み	3. expressing 表現する	
4. materialistic 物質的	5. opposite 反対の	6. philosophy 哲学	7. properly 適切に

A. After her cat died, the child went into ______.
B. I ______ the good advice she gave me.
C. A ______ person loves money more than people.
D. The men walked in ______ directions.
E. Her ______ of hard work has made her a success.
F. The painter enjoyed ______himself through his art.
G. He took his time completing the project because he wanted it done ______.

CD 12

"Be thankful for what you have; you'll end up having more. If you concentrate on what you don't have, you will never have enough." – ***Oprah Winfrey***

[1] Gratitude involves the exchange of positive feelings, and while it may seem to be a simple emotion, it is actually quite powerful, an essential part of human nature that is felt by all people of all cultures worldwide. Religion and **philosophy** have emphasized the importance of gratitude in daily life for thousands of years. Psychology has only recently understood its importance, with some psychologists now believing that it is the single most important human emotion, since it forms the base of our social life.

[2] When you are grateful, you do not focus on things that you do not have or on bad things; instead, you focus on what you do have, on the good things and the happy moments. And when we look closely, we find that our lives are full of such moments, things large and small. You can be grateful, for example, for the sun on your face, for your friends and family, for your ability to dream, for electricity or nature, for something that made you laugh – or for good health, since without health, you cannot experience life fully. Perhaps more importantly, when you get the feeling of gratitude, you should experience it, enjoy it completely, and allow that feeling to stay inside you for as long as you can; experience it, and enjoy it.

[3] Recently, a study was done on the effects of gratitude. People were put into three groups. The first group wrote a few sentences in a "gratitude journal" once a week for ten weeks: They wrote about recent things that they **appreciate** and for which they were grateful. The second group wrote of recent things that they found difficult and that made them unhappy. The third group wrote of anything that had an effect on them, both good and bad. The first group became 25 percent happier, had higher levels of energy and satisfaction, and experienced less stress. They also had fewer doctor visits and fewer headaches, colds, and other illnesses.

[4] In another study, people were given a week to **properly** thank someone who had done something special for them – something that was either important, kind, or wonderful. They would think about what that person had done and what it meant, and then had to write a letter **expressing** their gratitude. Finally, they visited the person and discussed the act of kindness with him or her. This last part was especially powerful because it was an "action" through which they gave back to someone who had helped them and were able to express their gratitude in person. After this, their happiness increased for a whole month. The study also found that those who just wrote the letter but did not send it, also experienced increased happiness, indicating that just expressing gratitude "works."

[5] Many people believe that happy people are more grateful. However, the **opposite** is true. If we are grateful, we become happy. Feeling gratitude cheers us up. Gratitude journals allow people to appreciate the things for which they are grateful, and those who write them show an increase in happiness of more than 10 percent. People who practice gratitude daily are more cheerful, and they have improved physical and mental health. Physically, they exercise more, have lower blood pressure, and evidence suggests that they may even live longer. Mentally, they are happier, more stable, better able to achieve their goals, more social, emotionally stronger, and suffer less stress and **depression**. Simple acts and expressions of gratitude are not only polite; but they can also result in our having more friends and better relationships. In contrast, those who feel ungrateful often end up disappointed, tend to be materialistic, and have lower self-esteem. Gratitude helps to balance our negative emotions, because we cannot have negative emotions and feel gratitude at the same time. Gratitude actually cancels out negative feelings. Gratitude changes lives.

"If the only prayer you ever say in your whole life is 'thank you,' that would suffice."
– Meister Eckhart

Active Outline: Choose the correct answer.

1. Religions have told of the importance of gratitude for ________ years.
   (many / hundreds of / thousands of)
   a. Recently, the importance of gratitude has been recognized by ________.
      (philosophy / religions / psychology)
2. There are many things to be grateful for, including ________.
   (health / food / a place to live / All of these.)
3. In a study on the effects of gratitude, people were divided into ________ groups.
   (two / three / four / five)
   a. The second group wrote of things that they ________ grateful for. (were / were not)
   b. The ________ group became 25 percent happier.
      (first / second / third / fourth / None of these.)
4. In another study, people had to express their ________ towards another person.
   (anger / gratitude / Both of these.)
   a. Those who did it were happier for a ________. (day / week / month / year)
5. Those who practiced gratitude daily had improved ________.
   (physical health / mental health / happiness / All of these.)
   a. Gratitude ________ those with stress. (helps / doesn't help)

Comprehension: Decide whether the statements are True (T) or False (F).

1. You should feel grateful for the small things. (True / False)
2. Happy people are not more grateful, but those who feel grateful are happier. (True / False)
3. It is possible to feel gratitude and to have a negative emotion at the same time. (True / False)
4. Those who are ungrateful are more likely to have lower self-esteem. (True / False)

Discussion / Writing: List six "small" things that you are thankful for.

1. ____________________ 2. ____________________
3. ____________________ 4. ____________________
5. ____________________ 6. ____________________

Opinion: Do you feel that you appreciate these things enough? Explain.

Reverse Questions: Write the questions that you would need to ask to get the answers below.

1. ____?

Answer: Gratitude has been spoken of in religion and philosophy for thousands of years.

2. ____?

Answer: For example, even if it is raining, you can be grateful for having an umbrella with you.

3. ____?

Answer: No. When you get that feeling of gratitude, you should enjoy it for as long as you can.

4. ____?

Answer: It was the first group in the study that became healthier and 25 percent happier.

5. ____?

Answer: No, actually it is the opposite. Those who are more grateful are overall happier.

Writing / Discussion: What are three things that you can do now to express your gratitude?

(Ex: *Call my grandparents and tell them how much they mean to me.*)

1. ______________ 2. ______________ 3. ______________

Opinion: Do you feel you show others your gratitude enough? When you do, does it make you and others happier? Explain.

Writing: Gratitude Journal.

A gratitude journal is a journal in which you write down things that you are grateful for that happened during the day. In one study, people who kept a weekly gratitude journal ended up 10 percent happier.

Write down six things (large or small) that recently happened to you that you are grateful for.

1. ____________________ 2. ____________________
3. ____________________ 4. ____________________
5. ____________________ 6. ____________________

Opinion: It was found that people who, before going to bed each night, wrote down three things in their gratitude journal that they were grateful for that day – and then reflected on it – had greater life satisfaction. They were happier, had lower stress levels, and slept better. How about you? Would you like to keep a "Gratitude Journal"? Explain.

Writing: Write a letter of appreciation to someone who has done something special for you, helped you, or supported you in some way. It could be a teacher, friend, parent, or anyone else. Thank this person.

1. Who is the person? *The person who I want to thank is* ____________________.
2. What did the person do for you? *The person helped me by* ____________________.
3. When, where, and why did the person help you? *The person helped me at the date and the place of* ____________________
____
____________________. *The reason I (asked / needed) the person's help was*
____
____________________.

Group Discussion: Discuss what happened in your groups. Also, consider how you will write your letter.

Notes: ____________________
____
____________________.

Writing: Begin your letter.

Dear ____________. *I want to thank you for when* ____________________
____________________.
You had helped me by ____________________
____
____
____________________.

Opinion: Did your happiness levels improve while you were writing the letter? Explain.

As I wrote this, I felt that my happiness levels (had / had not) increased. (It was especially strong when I wrote about / This is because) ____________________
____
____
____________________.

Make up two questions of your own to discuss with the other class members. Be creative !!

12. Processed Foods and Addiction

Pre-Reading Question: Can sugary / salty processed foods as candy, chocolate, potato chips be addictive?

Vocabulary: Fill in the blanks in the sentences below with the correct word.

1. addictive 中毒性のある	2. chemicals 化学物質	3. crave 強く望む
4. grease 油脂	5. narcotics 麻薬	6. overeat 食べ過ぎる
7. processed foods 加工食品	8. rotting 腐敗すること	9. texture 質感

A. The ______ were delicious, but they all had lots of ______ and oils.
B. Some foods are as ______ as ______.
C. This taste is interesting on my tongue and it has a unique ______.
D. The preservative ______ stopped the food from ______.
E. Jane would constantly ______ chocolate and would ______ it, which is why she gained weight.

13

"No one can exert … willpower over a biochemical drive that goes on every minute, of every day, of every year." – ***Dr. Robert H. Lustig***

[1] Food manufacturers create **processed foods** that are delicious and convenient for consumers and cheap for the companies to make. To better sell their products and increase their profits, the food companies create foods that not only fill you up, but also make you **crave** that food, so that you will buy and eat more of it. We all want delicious foods, so companies spend huge amounts of money to get their food scientists to come up with products that are as delicious as possible. This craving does not happen by chance; instead, a great deal of science and math goes into developing great tasting but **addictive** "junk" foods such as sodas, potato chips, cakes and cookies, pasta, and the like – in fact, just about every type of food that comes in a box, bottle, wrapper, or plastic container.

[2] To create processed foods, scientists put **chemicals** of all kinds in the food. These include preservatives to prevent the food from spoiling or **rotting**, coloring to make it look nice, flavoring to make it taste better, and **texture** to give it a certain "feel" in the mouth. These chemicals make food appealing to customers by not only covering up the bad taste, but also by causing people to want and eat more, even after they are full. This is the main reason why so many people cannot stop eating these foods, no matter how hard they try. Thus, people do not just eat these foods; they **overeat** them. Perhaps you have eaten a whole box of cookies

or whole carton of ice cream or drank a super-size soda without thinking about how quickly those things disappeared. This makes processed junk foods unlike real foods such as carrots or apples, which we know when to stop eating.

[3] Researchers at the University of Michigan have found that highly processed foods like pizza, chocolate, and French fries are the most addictive, while foods that are not processed – brown rice, salmon, carrots, apples, and beans – are not addictive. Real, natural foods are not addictive, which makes us wonder whether highly processed foods are "real" food. What makes processed foods so addictive is not the food itself, but the large amount of chemicals, salt, sugar, fat, unhealthy oils, and **grease** they contain. If these chemicals were removed, the food would not be addictive. It would taste terrible and no one would buy it.

[4] Processed foods have low nutrition levels compared to whole, natural, "real" foods, but they are so tasty that we eat much much more of them, so much in fact that they can make us sick. Some scientists and doctors believe that these foods are as addictive as some **narcotics**. These foods are compared to cigarettes, which also cause similar types of health problems, including liver disease, heart disease, high blood pressure, and possibly cancer. While no one is forcing people to eat those junk foods, our eating habits are very difficult to change: We cannot just stop eating altogether, and it is very difficult to know if the craving is due to real hunger or to addiction. This is why, in many ways, food addiction is more difficult to overcome than other addictions. The American diet contains over 70 percent processed foods. It is becoming increasingly difficult to avoid them, because they are sold everywhere: convenient stores, drug stores, supermarkets, and on the street. Natural, healthy foods such as fruits and vegetables are more expensive and often not so readily available.

"If it is made in a lab, then it takes a lab to digest." **– Kris Carr**

Active Outline: Choose the correct answer.

1. Food companies are NOT in business to make ________ food.
   (delicious / cheap / convenient / healthy)
   a. One way companies get people to buy more of their food is to get them to crave it. (True / False)
   b. Processed foods are created by ________. (nature / scientists)
2. The chemicals in processed foods include ________.
   (preservatives / flavoring / coloring / texture / All of these.)
3. One of the most addictive foods is ________. (salmon / brown rice / chocolate)
   a. Without the chemicals, the food would taste ________. (great / good / OK / awful)
4. Some health problems caused by these processed foods include ________.
   (high blood pressure / liver disease / heart disease / All of these.)
   a. Foods that are ________ are more common and easier to find in shops. (natural / processed)

Matching: Based on today's reading, match the sentence beginnings and endings.

1. Food companies are in business to ____ A. less nutrition than whole foods.
2. Processed foods usually come ____ B. believe that these foods are very addictive.
3. Some doctors and scientists ____ C. make their food tasty and cheap.
4. Processed foods are not made ____ D. because it's difficult to change our eating habits.
5. Junk foods are difficult to stop eating ____ E. in a garden.
6. Fruits and vegetables ____ F. are more difficult to find, and more expensive.
7. Processed foods have ____ G. in a box, bottle, wrapper, etc.

Fill in the blanks with one of these correct choices: a. preservatives, b. coloring, c. flavoring, d. texture.

To get a certain "feel" in the mouth, food companies put some 1. _________ in processed foods. It is the 2. _________ that allow the food to last for months, or even years. The 3. _________ makes the food look more appealing. And to get a certain taste, food companies add 4. _________.

Underline the products (bought in a supermarket) that are processed foods.

Donuts	Ketchup	Health Bars	An Apple
Jelly / Jam	Mango Yogurt	Orange Juice	Low Fat Cereal
Peanut Butter	Creamy Salad Dressing	Hamburger Buns	Eggs
Vitamin Water	A Banana	Banana Cookies	Baby Food

Reverse Questions: Write the questions that you would need to ask to get the answers below.

1. ____?
   Answer: The best way is to get their customers to overeat and crave their food.
2. ____?
   Answer: They must be cheap, easy to make, and last a long time.
3. ____?
   Answer: It said that foods such as pizza, chocolate, and French fries are the most additive.
4. ____?
   Answer: Both of them can cause liver disease, high blood pressure, and even cancer.
5. ____?
   Answer: Such foods are worse for you than cigarettes because you can't just stop eating.

Creative and Practical Writing: Tell your classmates about food addiction. *Be creative, and use your imagination!!*

I often go to a (supermarket / convenience store) to get my favorite processed (food / drink) called ______________. This food that I enjoy almost every (day / week) tastes ______________________________.
Unfortunately, today they did not have it, but instead I saw (a / some) ______________ ______________ and they looked ______________________, with the flavor of ______________. I've never seen that food before, but I decided to buy it, and it tasted ______________. Overall, I (am /am not) concerned about addiction to this type of food. The processed foods I often crave are ______________, and I will eat them (once / every) ______________.
I (do / often / sometimes / never) worry about how these foods affect my health because ____ ____.

Discussion:

I. The University of Michigan study looked at which foods are the most addictive. Which of the foods mentioned in the reading do you have the most problems with?

Opinion: Do you crave certain foods, even after eating a full meal?

II. What are some of your favorite processed foods? How often do you eat them?

Opinion: How can people escape being addicted to processed foods?

Debate: Write down and then discuss these questions with your classmates.

I. Dr. Lustig once said: "No one can exert … willpower over a biochemical drive that goes on every minute, of every day, of every year." Do you agree with this? Explain its discuss.

Opinion: Who is to blame for overeating? Should we blame McDonald's and other fast-food restaurants like it, which are found everywhere? Or should we blame the individual for overeating its food. Why?

II. Some argue that highly processed foods are not actually food (see paragraph 2), because food is supposed to provide nourishment and make us healthier. Is that all that food is for? Explain and discuss.

III. Give two reasons why addiction to cigarettes and addiction to "processed" foods are similar.

1. ______________________ 2. ______________________

Opinion: Are cigarette addiction and processed-food addiction similar? Explain.

Make up two questions of your own to discuss with the other class members. Be creative !!

13. Minimalism

Pre-Reading Question: What do you think is meant by "minimalist living"?

Vocabulary: Fill in the blanks in the paragraph below with the correct word.

1. clutter がらくたの山	2. decluttering 片づけ	3. distracting 目をそらさせる	
4. frustration 不満	5. miserable 悲惨な	6. possessions 所有物	7. society 社会

My desk had lots of (a) ______ on it, and the mess was (b) ______ me from what I really wanted to do. Then, looking around my room, I saw that my (c) ______ were all around me, and that this was causing me stress and (d) ______. So I would not become truly (e) ______, I began the process of (f) ______ my desk. I then tidied my room and, eventually, my entire house. I thought, perhaps if (g) ______ were to do this type of tidying on itself, the world would be a lot cleaner and much better organized.

CD 14

"There are two ways to be rich. One is by acquiring much,
and the other is by desiring little." – ***Jackie French Koller***

[1] Ryan Nicodemus was in his 20s, and very successful. He had everything he was supposed to have: an impressive job, a high salary, and a large house that had lots of stuff in it. But despite all his wealth, he felt increased stress and **frustration** and became very unhappy. To cheer himself up, he kept buying more and more expensive stuff: A big car, new electronics, fancy clothes, and beautiful things for the house that he rarely used. In other words, he tried to buy his way to happiness. All this stuff did not make things better, however; instead, it made things worse. Ryan paid for these things with his credit cards, which caused him to go into debt, and this went on for years. It seemed as if he was living for his material things, and he couldn't do what he really wanted to do. He had no time to think about his health, relationships, or passions. In the end, he became **miserable**, which led Ryan to speak to his also successful best friend, Joshua Millburn, who seemed truly happy.

[2] Joshua told Ryan about a new movement called minimalism. "Everything I owned wasn't making me happy, and worse, it was **distracting** me from the very things that brought me happiness," Joshua said. To move beyond this materialism, he decided to set a few clear, simple goals for himself and create a life with real purpose. Changing to a minimalist lifestyle was difficult at first. He found it especially hard to separate himself from his belongings. He got rid of one item a day for a month and soon realized that he didn't need thousands of **possessions** to feel happy. Gradually, it became easier to give things up. Eventually, he got rid of over 90 percent of everything he owned, and he became more grateful for the few items that remained.

[3] The philosophy of minimalism states that *less is more*. With *fewer* possessions, we spend *less* time and energy to clean and organize all our needless **clutter**. We have less stress, fewer distractions and frustrations. When we make space for things that are important to us, we gain *more*: *more* time, more meaningful relationships, *more* experiences, *more* personal growth, more opportunities to follow our passions.

[4] Ryan wanted to change, so he packed everything he owned into big boxes and gave himself three weeks to go through them all and decide what he really needed. Every day, he removed those items from the boxes that he really used like his toothbrush, some kitchenware, bed sheets, his favorite clothes, and some furniture. When deciding whether to toss an item he asked himself three questions: Does it have a purpose? Does it add value? Does it bring joy to his life? He decided that it's better to own three sweaters that he loved, instead of a closet filled with sweaters he didn't use. In three weeks, 80 percent of what Ryan owned was still in boxes. So he sold, gave away, and tossed the rest, including the excess furniture. His house changed from a cluttered mess to a warm and welcoming home with lots of open space. Ryan's view had changed, and for the first time, he felt truly rich.

[5] Joshua and Ryan are perhaps the most famous minimalists. There is no correct way to be a minimalist. Minimalism is not against having stuff, or about getting rid of everything you own. It is about owning the right stuff and simplifying your life. It is about not having attachment to your things and becoming free from the cycle of always buying the newest fashions, styles, and technology. We usually do not realize the amount of time, energy, and cost that is needed to take care of a big house, fancy clothes, and all the other items that we buy. Minimalism is most appealing to those in their 20s and 30s, perhaps because they want to be different from their parents, or perhaps because it's the opposite of what **society** encourages. But minimalism also appeals to retired people – they get rid of their "stuff" so that they can travel and do other exciting things.

[6] Minimalism may have as much to do with **decluttering** your mind as it does with decluttering your life! After you toss away the things you do not need, your emotions, mind, and spirit also get cleaned by getting rid of the old and making room for the new. Your life becomes fuller, and this is what minimalists mean by "less is more."

"Love people and use things, because the opposite never works." – ***Joshua Fields Millburn***

Active Outline: Choose the correct answer.

1. Before Ryan spoke with Joshua, he __________.
   (was successful / was unhappy / owned lots of stuff / All of these.)
2. Joshua __________ feel that his possessions made him happy. (did / did not)
   a. At first, Joshua __________ a hard time getting rid of what he owned. (had / did not have)
   b. Eventually, he became __________ grateful for the few items he still owned. (more / less)
3. With minimalism, you focus on __________.
   (possessions / distractions / wealth / what's important to you)
4. Ryan decided it's better to own __________ clothes. (a closet filled with / just a few)
5. There is only one way to live as a minimalist. (True / False)
   a. It is more important to own __________ stuff. (lots of / the right)
   b. Most people __________ realize how much time and effort and money all their stuff takes. (do / do not)
6. Minimalists are seeking a better __________. (fashion / stereo / house / life)

Comprehension:

1. The three things that Ryan asked himself when deciding whether to keep an item were: Does it have ________________? Does it add ______________? Does it bring ______________?
2. Changing to live as a minimalist is easy to do. (True / False)
3. If you live as a minimalist and have a book collection that you truly enjoy, you must still throw away _______ of your books. (all / most / some / none)
4. Minimalists usually live in empty houses and own almost nothing. (True / False)
5. What three words best express the philosophy of minimalism? (See paragraph 3.)
   The three words to best express the philosophy of minimalism are _____ _____ _____.
6. In your own words, define minimalism. *Minimalism is* ____.

Writing:

Does owning lots of stuff make you happier? Can you buy your way to happiness?
I (do / do not) think that owning lots of stuff makes you happier. This is because ____. *I (do / do not) think that it is possible to buy your way to happiness. This is because* ____.

Sentence Completion: Based on today's reading, fill in the blanks to complete the sentences.

1. Ryan was very _________ and had lots of _________; however, he was not ______________.
2. Ryan spoke to his best friend _________, who told him about ________________. Joshua had gotten rid of over _________________ of what he owned.
3. With minimalism, you spend less time ____________________, and you have more time for ______________________________.
4. Ryan decided to become a minimalist, too, so he packed up ________________ and gave himself three weeks to ____________________. His house changed from ____________________ to ________________.
5. Minimalism is most popular among those who are between the ages of ___ and ___ because ______________________________. It is also popular among those ____________________ because they would like to travel and do other exciting things.
6. Minimalism could have as much to do with decluttering your _______________ as it does with decluttering your _______________.

Critical Thinking:

Everything you own either brings you value – or brings you down. Name four items that you value, are meaningful to you, and gives you joy. Then name four items that do just the opposite.

Gives You Value: (Ex: *My favorite novel*)
1. ____________ 2. ____________
3. ____________ 4. ____________

Gives You No Value: (Ex: *My old Play Station*)
1. ____________ 2 . ____________
3. ____________ 4. ____________

Opinion: Give three reasons why people buy so much stuff that they don't need. (*Ex: Nonstop advertising*).

1. ________________ 2. ________________ 3. ________________

Questions / Discussions:

I. Do you think you own too much stuff? Explain.

I feel that I (do / do not) own too much stuff, and that it (is / is not) a problem with me. This is because ______________________________.

II. What percentage of your clothes do you wear regularly? About what percentage of your clothes could you throw away and not even notice that they are gone?

The percentage of clothes that I wear regularly is ___ percent. The percentage of clothes that I could toss out and not even notice that they are gone is ___ percent. This (is / is not) a problem because ______________________________.

Creative Writing: The Mind of a Minimalist. Pretend that you have decided to become a minimalist, and you will begin the process of decluttering your living space. How would you go about it?

1. *To begin, I must now look at everything I own, and imagine what I want my living space to look like. Before I decide whether to throw away something, I will ask myself a few questions: Does the item make my life better? Does the item have______________? Does it add______________? Does it bring ______________________________? If the item doesn't do these things, it gets removed.* (Hint: See paragraph 4 in the text.)
2. *First, I will tidy my room. I will take a big bag and toss all the clutter in my (closet / ______________) into it. The things that need to be thrown away will include ______________________________. The place in my (house / room / apartment) that causes me the most stress due to clutter is ______________ ______________. This is because ______________________________.*
3. *However, there are other things that I am uncertain if I want to throw away yet. For example, there is my ______________________________. This is because ______________________________. Perhaps I will put these items in boxes, and if I forget about them in ____________ months, I may toss them out, too. I (do / do not) feel that it will be possible to throw away 60 to 80 percent of everything I have within a year. This is because ______________________________ ______________________________. If I have less stuff, I (do / do not) believe that my level of stress will improve. This is because ______________________________ ______________________________.*

Opinion: Could you ever think like a minimalist? Explain and discuss.

Debate: Joshua once said, "Everything I owned wasn't making me happy, and worse, it was distracting me from the very things that did bring me happiness." Overall, do your possessions make you happy, or are they a distraction? Explain and discuss.

Overall, I think that all my possessions (make me happy / are a distraction). This is because ______________________________ ______________________________.

Make up two questions of your own to discuss with the other class members. Be creative !!

14. Flow

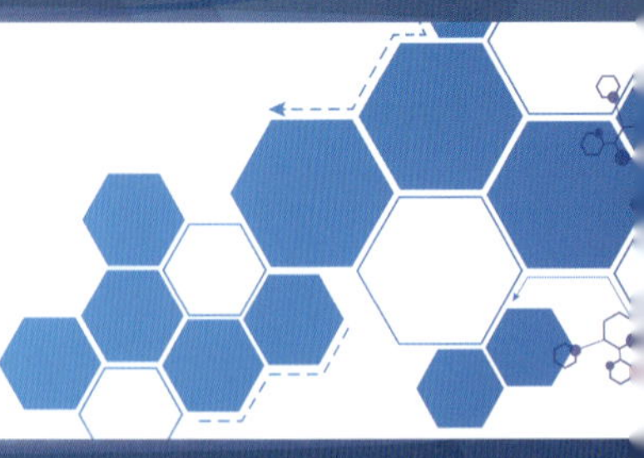

Pre-Reading Question: **How** does a person become happy? (Note that singing, dancing, watching television, and other such activities are not acceptable answers.)

Pre-Reading Question 2: What generally makes people happier, work or free time? Why?

Vocabulary: Match the sentence beginnings with their endings.

1. boredom 退屈	2. distractions 気を散らすもの	3. effortless 楽に
4. enthusiasm 熱意	5. involved 関わりを持つ	6. passive 受け身で
7. wander 彷徨い歩く		

1. There was a look of **boredom**
2. With all the **distractions** from outside, it
3. After a while, swimming became **effortless**,
4. There was **enthusiasm** in the air
5. Most residents spend their days on **passive**
6. He was so **involved** with his painting
7. Her mind would **wander** and she

____ a. and each stroke felt far easier.
____ b. that hours felt like minutes.
____ c. when our team tied the score.
____ d. had trouble focusing on the problem.
____ e. was difficult to focus on the lecture.
____ f. activities like watching television.
____ g. on all the children's faces.

"By stretching skills, by reaching toward higher challenges, such a person becomes an increasingly extraordinary individual." — ***Mihaly Csikszentmihalyi***

[1] The psychologist Mihaly Csikszentmihalyi wanted to find out what makes people happy. He traveled the world, asking people when they felt at their best. What he found was surprising. Everyone, whether athletes, painters, artists, pilots, engineers, chess players, and other people, said that they felt their best when what they were doing felt almost effortless. This happened regardless of gender, culture, or age. In 1969, Mihaly called this state *FLOW*, which he defined as "the state in which people are so involved with an activity that nothing else seems to matter."

[2] Mihaly found that those who love what they do are motivated simply because they enjoy it. People in flow can spend hours doing what they love without making any money or achieving any fame; all they need to do is to put their creativity and knowledge to good use. Mihaly wanted to understand **how** people enter and continue in this "flow state." The answer was that they should do something that they get joy from and then keep practicing that thing to get better and better at it. When people enter "flow," they are doing something important and are challenged just enough. If the task is too easy, it can lead to boredom. If it is too difficult, it can cause stress. Flow means achieving the right balance between your skill level and the challenge required to complete the task. As your skills improve, you can take on bigger challenges.

[3] Flow happens when you take risks, like speaking before a large crowd, doing something that is challenging like climbing Mount Fuji, solving a difficult problem, or even reading a novel – anything that leads to personal growth. One secret to finding flow is to find small ways to gradually improve what you are doing, and to express yourself in what you do, whether it is singing, dancing, cooking, and the like. When you are in a flow state, you are inspired, highly focused, and learn faster. Your mind does not **wander**, and you are not aware of any personal problems, surroundings, or anything else. You are so involved with the task that you have no worries or fear of failure. You lose track of time, and time goes faster: hours can pass by like minutes. You have clear goals and often get immediate feedback so that you know how well you are doing right away! You focus only on the challenging task at hand. You forget about everything else around you, do not even notice when you get hungry or tired. You are focused on the "now" (not the past or future). You feel free. You know when flow hits you. When the task is "difficult," it becomes effortless. **Enthusiasm** takes over. You are creative and productive, feel happy, and are in control.

[4] It may not always be a pleasant feeling while it is occurring; however, for example, runners in a race can feel weak and exhausted, or an actor on stage can be terrified of forgetting his or her lines. Yet these are often the best moments of their lives. Flow and happiness have nothing to do with ease. They are most often felt as you do something difficult, challenging, and perhaps even painful.

[5] To achieve flow, you should have no **distractions** (such as checking email, watching TV, etc.), since such interruptions will break your concentration and take you out of flow. But remember: the longer you are in flow, the easier it becomes to get distracted. When in flow, you should focus on a single task for as long as possible – at least 20 minutes. For example, if you are playing tennis, do your best to stay focused, win or lose. But being involved in a flow activity does not necessarily lead to a flow experience. A tennis player can become bored playing with a beginner – or frustrated when playing with someone far above his/her skill level.

[6] While people tend to believe that having lots of free time will make them happier than working, studies have found that the opposite is true. People have more opportunity to enter flow while at work. To reach a goal or complete a task, they solve challenges that are usually not too easy or too difficult. The person is concentrating, gets constant feedback, and has few distractions. During free time, on the other hand, we relax, but since we often have no clear goal, so the pleasures do not last very long. Doing something **passive**, like watching TV, rarely creates a state of flow because it usually does not lead to any personal growth. Research has shown that the best and happiest moments are not always easy; instead, people are happiest when they have a goal and are striving to reach it. Mihaly believed that creating more flow in life is the secret to happiness. And to find happiness, you have to find your own flow. Once you do, happiness will "flow" to you.

"Empty your mind, be formless. Shapeless, like water. If you put water into a cup, it becomes the cup. You put water into a bottle and it becomes the bottle. You put it in a teapot, it becomes the teapot. Now, water can flow or it can crash. Be water, my friend." – ***Bruce Lee***

Active Outline: Choose the correct answer.

1. Mihaly found that flow can happen with ________ people. (all / many / some / no)
2. People like what they do because of the ________ it gives them. (joy / money / difficulty)
   a. A task will put us into flow especially when it is ________. (needed / easy / difficult / a challenge)
3. When you are in flow, your mind ________ wander. (does / does not / may)
4. When a swimmer is in a race, in flow, his or her body ________ feel exhausted. (will / will not)
5. While in flow, it is important to ________ distractions. (have many / avoid)
6. People usually think that free time ________ make them happier than work. (will / will not)
   a. However, people are actually ________ happy during their free time. (more / less)

Reverse Questions: Write the questions that you would need to ask to get the answers below.

1. ____?

   Answer: People are happiest when they have a goal that they are striving to reach.

2. ____?

   Answer: No, flow only happens if we take on a challenge, a risk, or a difficult problem.

3. ____?

   Answer: Often hours go by in what feels like minutes, and we lose track of time.

4. ____?

   Answer: No, flow doesn't usually come during passive activities.

Comprehension: Short answers.

1. Name three things that happen when a person is in flow.

   1. ______________ 2. ______________ 3. ______________

2. Name three ideas from the article that you had never considered before. (*Ex: I had never considered that someone would ask people what makes them happy as Mihaly did.*)

   1. I had not considered ______________________________.
   2. I had not considered ______________________________.
   3. I had not considered ______________________________.

3. In your own words, describe what flow is. *I think that flow is* ______________________________

   ____.

Matching: Today's reading has six paragraphs. Match the paragraph numbers with the headings.

___ A. Flow has nothing to do with doing things that are easy.
___ B. How you can get into flow.
___ C. Mihaly wanted to better understand what makes people happy.
___ D. While people enjoy relaxing, having free time does not often lead to flow.
___ E. Distractions can prevent us from ever getting to flow.
___ F. To get into flow, the task cannot be too easy or too difficult.

Understanding:

Flow can happen as long as you do an activity that you enjoy and are learning from or getting better at such, as dancing, reading, playing chess, playing tennis, running, or being with a friend. Name three things you would like to get better at in the future.

1. ______________ 2. ______________ 3. ______________

Opinion: Which of these three things would give you the greatest amount of flow?

The activity that would give me the greatest amount of flow would be ______________.

This is because ____.

Writing:

1. Describe an experience you have had with flow when you were in high school or college.

   An experience I have had in (high school / college) was when ______________________________
   ______________________________. This took place about ________ year(s) ago. It was in the (town / city) of ______________________. What I remember about this experience was ______________________________
   ____
   ______________________________.

2. Describe a "flow" experience you have had with a relative or family member.

   An experience I have had with my (family / relatives) was when ______________________.
   What happened was ______________________________
   ______________________________.
   This took place about ________ year(s) ago. It was in the (town / city) of ____________.
   What I remember about this experience was ______________________________
   ____
   ______________________________.

3. *"The best moments in our lives are not the passive, receptive, relaxing times ... The best moments usually occur if a person's body or mind is stretched to its limits in a voluntary effort to accomplish something difficult and worthwhile."* – ***Mihaly Csikszentmihalyi (1990)***.

   When has your mind been stretched to its limits in an effort to do something worthwhile – when nothing else mattered to you, and you lost track of time?

   A "flow" experience I have done had was ______________________________.
   It was when I was ______________________________. What happened was __________
   ______________________________.
   It was in the (town / city) of ________________. What I most remember about the experience was ______________________________
   ____
   ______________________________.

Debate: Do you believe that flow is the secret behind finding happiness? If you can achieve your own flow, then will happiness come to you? Why or why not?

Make up two questions of your own to discuss with the other class members. Be creative !!

15. The Benefits of Being Scared

Pre-Reading Question: Can being scared improve your emotional health? Explain.

Vocabulary: Fill in the blanks in the sentences below with the correct word.

1. chemical 化学的な
2. confident 自信に満ちた
3. criticized 批判された
4. explore 探検する
5. expose さらす
6. immune system 免疫システム
7. nightmares 悪夢

A. In college, it is important to ______ different subjects that interest you.
B. There is a ______ in green tea that helps you relax and that also improves the ______.
C. There are nights when I have had bad dreams, even ______.
D. The young woman was extremely ______ when she got up to deliver her speech.
E. The student was ______ for wearing jeans in class.
F. The reporter wrote the article to ______ the president's lies.

"Do the thing you fear the most, and the death of fear is certain."
– Mark Twain

[1] Fear is as basic to humans as breathing and eating, and yet, it is still difficult to understand. Fear has allowed humans to survive for millions of years. When we become scared, our brain sends out a **chemical** signal that there is danger near, turning on a natural protection in our body that temporarily makes us quicker and stronger. That's the reason why when you are frightened you respond more quickly and either stand and fight or run away. Children as young as a few months old are afraid of falling and loud noises. Later in life, they learn to fear snakes, spiders, bees, skeletons, and other things.

[2] Some researchers believe that being scared improves not only our happiness, but also our health. It may also strengthen the **immune system**. Experiencing frequent small doses of fear is, in a way, "practice" for the brain to learn to better control itself in response to real threats. The more scared we are by watching scary movies, riding roller coasters, bungee jumping, sky diving, and the like, the stronger we become. When people face their own fears and **expose** themselves to things that frighten them (such as snakes, extreme sports, etc.), they often become stronger and, in time, overcome their fears.

[3] For example, scary movies can help us control our stress and fears. This is because we can better **explore** our own feelings of fear while we are perfectly safe. Since there is no real danger as we sit in the theater, we often experience joy when the movie ends. Watching a horror movie can burn off up to 200 calories. When two friends are frightened together, they get a feeling of closeness.

[4] Common fears include the fear of heights, flying, insects, and many others. Social fears include the fear of being closely watched, **criticized**, judged, or just being around other people. These social fears can also include the fear of public speaking, being on stage, running for class president, or trying out for a sports team. As a rule, with enough practice, we can get over these fears and become more **confident**. To aid this process, the brain releases a chemical that gives us pleasure. Of course, there are exceptions. Too much fear too soon can lead to greater stress, loss of sleep, or even **nightmares**.

[5] In general, men are more likely than women to enjoy scary movies and to do scary things. Perhaps men enjoy the feeling of defeating their own fear. Studies show that women find men who can control their emotions attractive. It is generally believed that it is more acceptable for women to show their feelings than it is for men. Perhaps this is why men find women who show their fears more attractive. Some people will even "test" or explore how much fear they can take to prove to themselves that they can handle it.

"What is needed, rather than running away or controlling or suppressing or any other resistance, is understanding fear; that means, watch it, learn about it, come directly into contact with it. We are to learn about fear, not how to escape from it." – ***Jiddu Krishnamurti***

Active Outline: Choose the correct answer.

1. Fear is considered a/an __________ emotion. (basic / advanced)
   a. When we experience fear, for a short time we become __________. (weaker / stronger)
   b. Children first develop a fear of __________. (snakes / falling / skeletons)
2. Fear is believed to be __________ for one's health. (good / bad / scary / unnecessary)
   a. Fear __________ help us to better respond to threats. (can / does not)
3. Watching scary movies __________ help us handle own stress better. (can / cannot)
   a. When two people watch a scary movie together, they often become __________. (closer / further apart)
4. Social fears include the fear of __________. (heights / being watched)
   a. If we can overcome our fear, we are more likely to become more __________. (shy / confident)
5. Women __________ attracted to men who can control their own fears. (are / are not)

Critical Thinking: What parts of today's reading do you agree with? What parts do you disagree with?

Agree:	Disagree:
1. ____________________	1. ____________________
2. ____________________	2. ____________________

Opinion: Overall, do you agree or disagree with the ideas presented in the article? Why?

Matching: Today's reading has five paragraphs. Match the paragraph numbers with the headings.

____ A. How males and females differ in their reactions to fear.
____ B. Fear as a basic human emotion.
____ C. The different kinds of fear.
____ D. The benefits of being scared while we are perfectly safe.
____ E. How fear can help us become stronger.

Writing / Conversation:

1. What is it in scary movies that frightens us?

   Opinion: Describe and discuss a scary movie you have seen.

2. How would you compare Japanese and American scary movies? Which are scarier? Which do you prefer? Why?

3. Do you think that being scared is good for your health? Why or why not?

   Opinion: If being scared really is "good for you," should you then make an effort to be scared more often? If so, how would you do this? If not, why not?

True or False: Decide whether the statements are True (T) or False (F).

____ 1. Fear has helped humans to survive.
____ 2. When we become scared, chemicals in the brain relax us.
____ 3. Riding in a roller coaster may briefly make us stronger.
____ 4. When we avoid our fears, we become stronger.
____ 5. Scary movies cannot help us explore our feelings of fear.
____ 6. It is impossible to experience joy when we are exploring our feelings of fear.
____ 7. One cannot experience too much fear.
____ 8. Men find it attractive when women control their emotions.

Creative Storytelling: Hollywood is calling!

A famous Hollywood producer wants you to come up with a really frightening character for a new horror movie. Your character must be different from any scary-movie characters ever before seen. Create a scary character. *Be creative, and use your imagination!!*

This character's name is ________________. It is a (person / object / __________) that looks like ____.

What is scary when you look at this character is that ______________________ ______________________. What is makes this character so dangerous is that ______________________ ______________________. Since ______________________, the best way to defend yourself against this "thing" is to ______________________ ______________________. The scariest scene in the movie is when ______________________ ______________________.

My Feedback: Give feedback on your classmates' "characters." Write down some questions.

______________________? ______________________?
______________________? ______________________?

Opinion: Whose character was the scariest and most interesting?

The person in my group whose character was the scariest and most interesting is ______________________. This is because ______________________ ______________________.

Discussion:

I. What are you most afraid of? Describe this fear and how you think you might "defeat" it? (Ex: *I am most afraid of going to the dentist because ...*)

I am afraid of ______________________. The first time I experienced this fear was when I was __________ years old. What happened was ______________________ ______________________.

A possible way for me to get over this fear is by ______________________.

II. Tell a partner about your greatest fear and ask that person to help you "defeat" it. What did you learn about yourself from your partner? Was the advice helpful? Note: When others ask you to help them deal with a fear they have, first, find out why they feel that way and when the fear started. Then try to change their thinking from negative to positive.

What I learned after discussing my fear with my partner was ______________________ ______________________.

Debate: Write down and then discuss these questions with your classmates.

I. Name three of what you think are the scariest movies ever made.

II. Which do you prefer, doing something that gives you a thrill or reading a book / solving Sudoku? Why?

Make up two questions of your own to discuss with the other class members. Be creative !!

16. Social Media and the Fear of Missing Out (FoMO)

Pre-Reading Question: Do social media such as Facebook, etc. help or harm mental health? Why?

Vocabulary: Fill in the blanks in the sentences below with the correct word.

1. brag 威張る、誇示する	2. compare 比較する	3. compete 競う
4. concentrate 集中する	5. idealized 理想化された	6. unintentionally 意図しないで

A. She would often ______ about how her play won the game.
B. Four teams will ______ to win.
C. He would often ______ give the wrong information.
D. Can you ______ with the music playing?
E. He ______ his past as wonderful, when it actually wasn't.
F. How would you ______ Tokyo and Osaka?

17

"Comparison is the thief of joy."
– Theodore Roosevelt

[1] There are many wonderful things about social media. They can provide us with information of all kinds quickly and easily. They have become an important communication tool and have changed the way we communicate, allowing us to be in touch with others, anywhere, anytime, and to get immediate feedback. No wonder we use social media so often. In 2017, Americans checked their cell phones on average 80 times a day, and spend an average of 135 minutes on social media every day, especially on Facebook, the world's most popular social-media site.

[2] Social media allows us to easily keep in touch with others. However, if we don't hear from people after a little while, we wonder what they are doing, and what we are "missing out" on. This is called the "Fear of Missing Out," or FoMO. Those with FoMO check their social media sites every chance they get. Teenagers may spend several hours a day on social media. One in four say they are online nearly all the time. They are trying to keep up with all the information that is available. But that's impossible, because the information changes all the time. Teenagers who spend more than just two hours a day on social media sites are more likely to get lower grades, drink and smoke, and have difficulty sleeping. The overuse of social media not only changes the way we communicate; it can actually change the brain itself, making it more difficult for us to concentrate.

[3] On social media, people often but perhaps, unintentionally, present themselves not in the most truthful way, posting only their best possible idealized self. This can lead us to assume that others are happier, and to **compare** ourselves constantly to them – to tell ourselves that we are happier and more successful than our friends or other people we know. For example, perhaps you see on Facebook that your friends are eating in a nice restaurant while you are having a plain meal at home. Or your friends post pictures of themselves having fun at Tokyo Disneyland, while you are working long hours at your part-time job. This can force people to "**compete**" with others. Some will constantly **brag**, always posting only how wonderful things are, showing only their best online photos, making only attractive comments, giving out fake success stories trying to get the most likes – while never posting their unhappy moments or failures. The problem is that their online life is separate from their real life, and this cycle can be difficult to stop. When we compare lives online, we feel our life is duller than others' – even if it's not true at all – and we become less happy. Even if your friends are doing something dull together, and you are doing something really fun, you can still end up feeling worse about yourself. You think that something important might happen within your group of friends, and since you won't be there to experience it with them, your stress and worry increase because you are "missing out."

[4] Of course, social media does not make everyone unhappy. But we need to question our relationship with it. Is it healthy? You need to pay attention to your own online use and understand the possible problems it causes. Being on social media is not as satisfying as being with other people. Those who overuse social media are often less happy, and may eventually have difficulty communicating. They may even become withdrawn and unsocial. According to experts, when you use social media, you should not compare yourself to others. Rather, you should use social media as a tool to meet your friends at a later time.

"Technology has become the center of our social world, compelling us to always keep checking in to see what we're missing." ***– Larry Rosen, PhD***

Active Outline: Choose the correct answer.

1. Social media ________ changed the way we communicate. (has / has not)
2. People with FoMO check their social media account ________.
   (when they wake up / while eating meals / before they sleep / whenever they can)
   a. There is a ________ of information online, and it changes a ________.
      (little, little / little, lot / lot, lot)
   b. Those who spend too much time online can have difficulty with ________.
      (grades / stress / sleeping / All of these.)
   c. Overuse of the Internet ________ lead to changes in the brain. (may / cannot)
3. One problem is that people ________ present themselves in the most accurate way.
   (tend to / do not always)
   a. Comparing yourself to others online ________ a good thing to do. (is / is not)
   b. People may post how great things are, when they are not. (True / False)
4. Everyone who uses social media will eventually become unhappy. (True / False)
   a. If we use social media too often, we may have difficulty with ________.
      (English / being social / TOEIC tests)
   b. Rather than being on social media, one way to make your life better is to ________.
      (compare yourself to others / avoid people / study English / meet your friends)

Critical Thinking:

1. What are some of the positive and negative effects of social-media use?

Positive:
1. ______________
2. ______________
3. ______________

Negative:
1. ______________
2. ______________
3. ______________

Opinion: Is your relationship with social media healthy? Why or why not?

2. What are some problems that someone with FoMO could have?

List three problems given in the article.
1. ______________
2. ______________
3. ______________

List three problems not given in the article.
1. ______________
2. ______________
3. ______________

Opinion: Which social-media site do you use most often – Facebook, Twitter, or something else? Why do you use it?

Writing:

When were you on social media and felt happy? When did you feel stressed? Explain.

1. *A time I felt good while on social media was when ______________.*

   For example, what happened was ______________.

2. *A time I felt stressed on social media was when ______________.*

   For example, what happened was ______________.

Opinion: On a scale of 1 to 10, 10 being highest, how serious a problem is FoMO for you?

On a scale of 1 to 10, 10 being the highest, I think that FoMO for me rates a ____. This is because ______________ ______________.

Matching: Today's reading has four paragraphs. Match the paragraph numbers with the headings.

____ A. How can you use social media in a healthy way?
____ B. The importance of social media.
____ C. How do people describe themselves on social media?
____ D. What are some problems with FoMO?

Creative / Critical Thinking:

What is the article missing? What information and ideas would you add to make it more complete?

I think that what is missing from the article is that ______________________

____

____

______________________.

Writing / Discussion / Presentation: (answer a few of these).

I. Why (do / don't) you use social media? Give examples.

____

____

II. Do you try to get more positive comments, "likes," "followers," or "friends"? Explain.

____

____

III. How many times a day do you use social media? How do you feel after you use it?

____

____

IV. Many people believe that they had more fun before social media existed, and that people are now missing out on fun because they are so glued to their cell phone.
1. Do you agree? Explain. 2. Would you prefer that social media did not exist? Explain.

____

____

Debate: Write down and then discuss these questions with your classmates.

I. One study found that overall, the more time people spend on social media, the more depressed and even miserable they become. Do you agree, and if not, why not?

II. On a scale of 1 to 10, 10 being highest, how much of a problem is FoMO for some of your friends? For your generation as a whole? Explain.

Make up two questions of your own to discuss with the other class members. Be creative !!

17. Gender-Neutral Parenting

Pre-Reading Question: Why do boys like blue and girls like pink?

Vocabulary: Fill in the blanks in the sentences below with the correct word.

1. advertisements 広告	2. evolution 進化	3. diapers おむつ
4. nurturing 育てること	5. pregnant 妊娠して	6. stereotyping ステレオタイプ

1. When walking to work, I saw lots of (a) ______ for (b) ______ and other items for (c) ______ women.
2. Women are thought to be more (d) ______ and are supposed to raise children. I wonder if this is a result of (e) ______or is it just unfairly (f) ______ others.

CD 18

*"I am saying to the world: 'Please can you just let Storm discover for him or herself what he or she wants to be?'" – **Kathy Witterick, Storm's mother***

[1] When a woman is **pregnant**, the first thing people usually ask is whether the child is a boy or girl. But does it really matter? Society expects people to act in a certain way based on gender, and their expectations of babies are no different. As children, boys are expected to be "strong," tough, and independent, while girls are "princesses" and are raised to be caring and **nurturing**. We tell boys not to cry, but comfort crying girls. In one study, a baby was dressed first in blue and then in pink. When the baby was in blue, people were more physical with it, playing more active games. But when that same child was wearing pink, people gave it dolls to play with and gently calmed it. Baby boys' rooms are often decorated in blue or green and have sports equipment or toy guns in them. Baby girls' rooms, in contrast, are decorated in pink, purple, or other bright colors, and have lots of cute toys and dolls in them. By the age of two, most boys will avoid anything pink. Girls are likely to have many pink toys. Many experts say that this is the beginning of children favoring their own gender.

[2] Are these differences due to culture or **evolution**? For centuries, both sexes wore white dresses until the age of six. In the early 1900s, one magazine declared that pink is for boys and blue is for girls. **Advertisements** and famous department stores told parents that pink is "stronger," a "boyish" form of the adult "manly" color of red. Blue, meanwhile, was said to be "delicate" and blue dresses were considered especially feminine. But in the 1950s, things changed. Companies made and advertised blue for boys and pink for girls. The colors could have gone either way. In the 1960s, to increase profits, makers offered different colored—and more expensive toys—to the different genders. In the 1970s, this gender marketing decreased, but in 1985, it became popular again, with toys, clothing, gifts, and even **diapers** being sold in blue for boys and in pink for girls. Sporting goods, tools, toy cars, and darker-colored clothes were advertised for boys, while dolls, furniture, stuffed animals, and brightly colored clothes were advertised for girls.

[3] Not too long ago, one Canadian couple believed that gender **stereotyping** was harmful, so they decided to raise their child named Storm as gender neutral. They felt that society and too many parents were pushing their gender-biased values on their children. During the first five years, Storm did not watch television and wore both male and female clothing. No one was told whether Storm was male or female – no other parents, teachers, or even the child's friends. Even the grandparents complained of the difficultly of explaining to others that their grandchild was more of an "it" than a "he" or "she." Storm decided whether to play with cars or dolls. As Storm's mother put it, "Why would you want to (put) people into boxes? Gender affects what children wear and what they play with, which shapes the kind of person they become." While some thought that it was a good idea, others thought it was strange and that the couple were crazy.

[4] It may be impossible to raise a child completely as gender neutral, but those who favor at least trying it argue that raising a child as one gender limits the child. When children are not thus limited, they are exposed to a greater range of activities, experiences, and creativity. They can explore their real interests. When they grow up, they are able to communicate better with the other gender, be more confident, and be better leaders. Females can become better at science and math and get more involved in politics or become company presidents. Males can express their thoughts and feelings better, understand female viewpoints, do more around the house, and be better fathers. The long-term effects on a child that is raised as gender neutral are not known. While some people believe that gender-neutral parenting allows children to have greater experiences and find their true identities, others fear it could confuse them or even separate them from society.

Flowers are red young man,
green leaves are green.
There's no need to see flowers any other way
than the way they always have been seen.

– Harry Chapin, 1978

Active Outline: Choose the correct answer.

1. People are often expected to act in a certain way based on their gender. (True / False)
   a. If a baby girl is dressed in blue, people are likely to treat her like a ________. (boy / girl)
   b. Boys are ________ to buy a pink airplane. (likely / not likely)
2. Centuries ago, very young children wore ________ dresses. (blue / pink / red / white)
   a. In the early 1900s, ________ was the "manly" color for adult males. (blue / pink / red / white)
   b. In those days, pink was the recommended color for ________ to wear.
   (men / women / boys / girls)
   c. Blue for boys, pink for girls first became popular in the ________.
   (early 1900s / 1950s / 1960s / 1980s)
3. Storm was raised as a ________. (male / female / Neither of these.)
   a. Storm's mother felt that limiting Storm to one gender would limit the child's ________.
   (choices / future / personality / All of these.)
4. Children raised gender-free can have ________ experiences. (more / fewer)

Critical Thinking:

1. Give three examples how society encourages male and female differences.
   1. ____.
   2. ____.
   3. ____.

   Opinion: Does society *encourage* differences in gender? Explain.

   I think that society (does / does not) encourage differences in gender. This is because

   ____

   ____.

2. What are some of the reasons for and against raising a gender-neutral child?

For raising a gender-neutral child.	Against raising a gender-neutral child.
Ex: The child will see all colors as equal.	*Ex: The child may become confused.*
1. ____________________	____________________
2. ____________________	____________________
3. ____________________	____________________

   Opinion: Should parents dress their babies and children as male or female or in gender-neutral clothing? Or should they allow the children to express themselves anyway they like? Explain.

Writing:

1. Do gender differences in children's dress, toys, and colors limit children? Explain.

   I feel that gender differences (do / do not) limit children. This is because ____________

   ____

   ____.

2. As a child, what were some of your favorite toys or activities? Were they gender specific? How do you think these influenced your adult personality or outlook?

   When I was a child, some of my favorite (toys / activities) were ____________.

   What I liked about them most was ____________________.

   (All / Most / Some / None) of my (toys / activities) were gender specific. For example,

   ____

   ____.

   I (feel / don't feel) that these influenced my adult personality. This is because ________

   ____

   ____.

Sentence Unscramble: Put the words in the correct order to make complete sentences.

1. upon / way / supposed / their gender. / to behave / in a certain / People are / based

   ____

2. pink / blue bottles. / food / or / is / The / in / baby / sold

   ____

3. differences / as early as / learn gender / age two. / might / Children

   ____

4. dolls to play with. / in pink, / When the / was / people / child / likely / were more / to give it

____

5. the / the / the / aisle / aisle / has / has / blue / pink / girls' toys. / boys' toys, and / store, / In

____

Writing / Discussion: Answer and then discuss the questions with your classmates.

I. Do you think there are natural differences in how genders see colors and toys, or is it just a marketing trick? Explain?

____

____

Opinion: Are we limiting children's choices, and preventing them from exploring the activities and interests of the other gender? Explain.

II. How well do you communicate with the opposite sex? What problems do you have? Explain.

____

____

Opinion: If you had been raised as gender neutral, do you think you would communicate with the opposite sex better? Why?

III. Some people believe that everyone has a male and female self. Describe something that you like doing that is considered the opposite of what your sex is "supposed" to like.

____

____

Opinion: What skill that the opposite gender has would you like to better at? Why?

Debate: Write down and then discuss these questions with your classmates.

I. If you decided to raise a gender-neutral child, what would be the three most important factors for you to consider? Explain.

1. ____________________. *This is because* ____________________.
2. ____________________. *This is because* ____________________.
3. ____________________. *This is because* ____________________.

II. What is your opinion of gender-neutral parenting?

Make up two questions of your own to discuss with the other class members. Be creative !!

18. The Science of Altruism

Pre-Reading Question: Why do people cooperate and help each other?

Vocabulary: Fill in the blanks in the sentences below with the correct word.

1. altruism 利他主義	2. empathy 共感	3. human evolution 人間の進化
4. reputation 評判	5. spouse 結婚の相手	6. trust 信頼

A very wealthy man had a (a) ______ who was very kind. She wanted to build hope and (b) ______ in the community. Helping others is an example of what is called (c) ______. The wealthy man and his wife made many friends and had an excellent (d) ______. They understood people's feelings and had great (e) ______ for others. Perhaps (f) ______ intends for us to not be selfish but rather to help one another.

CD 19

"Love your neighbor as yourself."
– Leviticus 19:18

[1] **Altruism** means "living for others." This quality can be considered a higher form of personal development. Altruism is the desire to help others – as individuals or by working for society – rather than to just selfishly look out for oneself. Many scientists believe that altruism is deeply embedded within human nature. Religions and cultures everywhere teach that altruism is an important moral virtue. Humans are social beings and need to help each one another to survive. When we help others, pleasure chemicals that make us feel good and even happier are released deep within our brain. This is why helping others gives us such great satisfaction. With altruism, we help others without expecting any help – or anything else – back. Everyone benefits when we act altruistically, even if there is cost to ourselves.

[2] We feel closer to those we help. Through altruism, we build **trust**, connections, and a good **reputation**. We grow emotionally, and others around us become happier and kinder. People see us as more honest, friendlier, and more helpful, and thus we have a greater chance of making even more friends. Others are more likely to cooperate with us, return us favors, or help us in the future if we are having trouble.

[3] When they are doing a task, people are more successful while cooperating rather than when competing. When students study together for a project, they are more likely to be more social and have better relationships. People who cooperate have better physical health, suffer fewer aches and pains, and are emotionally stronger. Being altruistic is important when we are seeking a **spouse.** In many studies, women have found altruistic men more attractive, better at dating, and more suitable as marriage partners.

[4] Studies show that we are more likely to cooperate with those who are part of our family or our group or circle, or with people we are likely to see again. When you see someone who is suffering, you naturally feel **empathy** and perhaps a desire to help him or her. Young children will automatically try to help others out of true concern for them. Animals show altruism to other animals too, and overall, animals that cooperate live longer and are more productive than those that do not. Monkeys share their food and help their sick and injured. Wild dogs and wolves bring meat back to the entire pack, giving food to those who did not kill the meat themselves. Birds protect an unrelated bird's young from other animals that aim to harm or eat them. Fish help other fish clean their nest. A rat in a lab becomes stressed when it sees another rat being shocked or in pain.

[5] When we give, others are more likely to give back. When we are kind, others are more likely to be kind back. When we see an act of kindness, we get a warm feeling inside. This is a result of our **human evolution**. It proves that humans have evolved to cooperate, to help one another, to try to make the world a better place. This does not mean that people are more altruistic than selfish. Humans can act either way. So perhaps our greatest challenge is for people to act for a greater good.

"Many illnesses can be cured by the one medicine of love and compassion. These qualities are the ultimate source of human happiness, and the need for them lies at the very core of our being."

– Dalai Lama

Active Outline: Choose the correct answer.

1. Scientists believe that helping others __________ natural. (is / is not)
2. When we help others, people see us as more honest. (True / False)
3. People feel better when they __________ with each other. (compete / cooperate)
   a. Those who are altruistic have better physical and emotional health. (True / False)
4. Animals do not show altruism. (True / False)
5. When you are kind, others are __________ likely to be kind back. (more / less)
   a. People cannot be both altruistic and selfish. (True / False)

Critical Thinking:

1. Give three examples of a time when you gave something to or helped someone and three examples of a time when you received help or something else.

Gave to or helped someone:	Received help or something else:
1. ____________________	____________________
2. ____________________	____________________
3. ____________________	____________________

Opinion: Overall, which has given you the most pleasure, giving or receiving? Why?

Overall, when I (give / receive) something, I get more pleasure. For example, __________

____

____.

2. Give examples of altruistic and selfish behavior that you have seen in the movies or on TV.

Altruistic behavior:	Selfish behavior:
1. ______________________	______________________
2. ______________________	______________________
3. ______________________	______________________

Opinion: How did you feel as you watched the altruistic and selfish behavior?

When I saw the altruistic behavior, I felt ______________________.

When I saw the selfish behavior, I felt ______________________.

Sentence Unscramble: Put the words in the correct order to make complete sentences.

1. one another. / are / social beings / who need / People / to help

____

2. feel / This / happiness / why we / while / others. / helping / is

____

3. inside. / a warm / After / helping / we / feeling / others, / get

____

4. to / When / likely / more / helping others, / make friends. / we are

____

5. are / with us. / more / cooperate / Others / to / likely

____

6. see / you may / another person / to help. / suffering, / strong desire / When you / have a

____

7. and could / Helping / you more / you find / attractive / others makes / help / a spouse.

____

Creative Discussion and Presentation.

Your group has decided to help some circle or organization. How will you help them?

1. Who will be helped? ______________________.
2. Why do they need help? ______________________.
3. Where and when will you help them? *It will take place at* __________ *on the date of* _____.
4. Name three things that you will do to help them.

   Three things we will do to help the circle or organization include:

   (1) ______________________.

   (2) ______________________.

   (3) ______________________.
5. How will your help benefit the organization? ______________________.

6. Now pretend that you have already given the help. Explain what happened.
   While doing ______________ *what happened was* ______________
   ______________.
   However, there was problem(s) when ______________
   ______________.

7. Was your help successful or beneficial? Why or why not?
   It (was / was not) successful, because ______________
   ____
   ______________.

Conversation Activity: There are times when we act selfish and other times we act altruistic.

Write about a time when you were selfish.
A time when I was selfish was when ______________
____
______________.

Write about a time when you were altruistic.
A time when I was altruistic was when ______________
____
______________.

Debate: Write down and then discuss these questions with your classmates.

I. Today's reading states that religions and cultures everywhere teach the importance of helping others. Give an example or two of a religious or cultural "lesson" on altruism.

II. In general, do you think that Japan is a more altruistic or a more selfish society? Why?
I feel that overall, Japan is a more (altruistic / selfish) society. This is because ______________
____
______________.

Opinion: Overall, are people more altruistic or more selfish? Why do you think so?

Make up two questions of your own to discuss with the other class members. Be creative !!

19. Counterfactual Thinking

Pre-Reading Question: Recently, scientists looked at video of Olympic Games winners as they were awarded their medals. Who generally looked happier, the silver or bronze medal winners? Why?

Vocabulary: Match the words in bold with their endings.

1. compare 比較する	2. consider 考える	3. disappointment 落胆
4. expected 予想された	5. scientists 科学者たち	

1. When you **compare** yourself to another, you
2. When we **consider** how to improve something,
3. When we feel **disappointment**, we are
4. When something is **expected**,
5. **Scientists** are

____a. we believe it will happen.
____b. experts in a field of study.
____c. we think carefully about it.
____d. measure yourself against that person.
____e. upset or sad because of some failure.

20

"I've missed more than 9000 shots in my career. I've lost almost 300 games. 26 times, I've been trusted to take the game winning shot and missed. I've failed over and over and over again in my life. And that is why I succeed."
– Michael Jordan

[1] Recently, some **scientists** looked at the happiness levels of Olympic Games medal winners and noticed something unusual. While the silver is a higher level medal than the bronze, the bronze medal winners were almost always happier. The scientists concluded that this was because the silver medal winners imagine what might have been – how close they came to winning a gold medal. In other words, they **compare** themselves to the gold medal winner, perhaps thinking, "If I only had …" or "Why didn't I just …" The bronze medal winners, however, imagine not getting anything at all. They are happy to have just gotten a medal. This type of thinking is called counterfactual thinking.

[2] Counterfactual thinking, the study of which began in 1982, comes when we imagine how things could have turned out differently from what actually happened. For example, if you had not entered this university, how would things be different for you? Counterfactual thinking is when we ask ourselves "What if …" "If only …" "What would …," and similar questions. For example, "What if Tokyo were further south, how warm would its summers be?" or "If the fish had been cooked longer, maybe I wouldn't have gotten sick." We all ask questions like these from the time we are children, no matter what the country, language, or culture. Counterfactual thinking occurs more often when something goes wrong than when something goes right. There are different types of counterfactual thinking, including upward, downward, additive, and subtractive.

[3] Upward counterfactual thinking comes when we **consider** what we should have done and ask ourselves how things could have been better. We think, "I shouldn't have ..." "I could have ..." or "I didn't correctly ...," and the like. Sports teams consider what they did wrong after a losing game. Businesses consider how a new product might have sold better. Students are unhappy with a "B" grade if they had **expected** an "A." They might think "I should have studied harder" or "I should had gone to sleep earlier instead of watching YouTube." Although we feel some **disappointment**, upward counterfactual thinking helps us learn and improve, whether it's studying for exams, searching for a job, choosing what to eat or where to travel, and in many other situations. But too much counterfactual thinking can cause stress, disappointment, and even depression.

[4] Downward counterfactual thinking: This type of thinking is less common than upward thinking. Here, we consider how things could have been worse – and feel grateful. For example, if you had an accident and broke your leg, you might be grateful that you didn't need additional surgery. Or perhaps you are happy with a "B" grade, because you had expected a "C" or even a failing grade. With this type of thinking, while things are not great, they could have been worse. We feel better about what happened, but at the same time we are less likely to learn from our mistakes or to improve.

[5] We usually consider counterfactuals when we think about important happenings. While we cannot change the past, we know that something similar could happen to us in the future. Thus, even the small changes we make in our behavior can completely change the outcome of a future event, for better or for worse. Understanding this psychology can help us better understand ourselves and perhaps even avoid future problems and mistakes.

"This is the shiniest bronze medal you will ever see. Ever!"
– Brendan Hansen, London 2012 Olympics.

Active Outline: Choose the correct answer.

1. The ________ medal is lower than the ________. (bronze, silver / silver, bronze)
   a. Scientists found that the ________ medal winner was overall happier. (silver / bronze)
   b. The ________ medal winner would often compare to the gold medal winner. (silver / bronze)
2. With counterfactual thinking, we consider what could have been ________. (different / the same)
   a. ________ people do counterfactual thinking. (All / Most / Some / Few / No)
   b. It happens most often when something goes ________. (well / not well)
3. With upward counterfactual thinking, we think of how things could become ________. (better / worse)
   a. This helps us, since it ________ as individuals. (makes us feel better / allows us to improve)
4. With downward counterfactual thinking, we think of how things could become ________. (better / worse)
   a. This helps us, since it ________ as individuals. (makes us feel better / allows us to improve)
5. Most people think of counterfactuals after ________ events. (everyday / important)
   a. With counterfactual thinking, we can ________. (learn / change what happened / correct the past / All of these. / None of these.)

Comprehension: Decide if the following are upward (U) or downward (D) counterfactual thinking.

1. The silver medal winner was (more / less) happy, and did (U/D) thinking.
   This is because ____.

2. The bronze medal winner was (more / less) happy, and did (U/D) thinking.
   This is because ____.

3. The soy sauce splashed all over my tie ________
   a. but at least it didn't stain my shirt. (U/D)   b. so the next time, I'll eat more slowly. (U/D)

4. After I was in a car accident, I realized that I ________
   a. should have taken another way to work. (U/D)   b. would be back at school within a week. (U/D)
   c. should not use Twitter while driving. (U/D)   d. did not need surgery. (U/D)

5. The job interview didn't go well, (and/but) ______
   a. I need to prepare a better resume. (U/D)   b. next interview, I will go to sleep earlier. (U/D)
   c. I am glad that I made it through. (U/D)   d. it was good experience. (U/D)

6. Create Your Own: ____.
   a. (upward) ____________________.   b. (downward) ____________________.
   c. (upward) ____________________.   d. (downward) ____________________.

Additive Counterfactual Thoughts: With this type of counterfactual thinking, you ***add*** something that you should have done, but didn't. For example, to lose weight, you might add exercise.

Subtractive Counterfactual Thoughts: With this type of counterfactual thinking, you ***subtract*** or take away something you did. For example, if you are trying to lose weight, you might regret (or subtract) eating a piece of chocolate cake.

Counterfactual Thoughts: Decide if the following are additive (A) or subtractive (S) counterfactual thinking.

1. Last year in college, I should have ______
   a. taken a math class. (A/S)   b. joined the tennis club. (A/S)
   c. not taken a math class. (A/S)   d. not joined the tennis club. (A/S)

2. Today, I would not be sick if only I had ______
   a. taken the medicine. (A/S)   b. exercised more. (A/S)
   c. not drunk so much sake. (A/S)   d. not gone running in the rain. (A/S)

3. I would not have injured myself while playing baseball if only I had ______
   a. remember to tie my shoes. (A/S)   b. not run so fast. (A/S)
   c. not fallen down. (A/S)   d. kept my eye on the ball better. (A/S)

4. Create your own: The last time I was with friends, we would have had more fun if we had ______
   a. (additive) ____________________.   b. (subtractive) ____________________.
   c. (additive) ____________________.   d. (subtractive) ____________________.

Short Answers:

1. How did you first meet your best friend? What would have stopped this from happening?
   I first met my best friend (while / at) ______________________. What happened was ____. What would have stopped me from meeting my best friend is ______________________________ ____.

2. What would have made last Christmas or New Year's better?
   What would have made that time better was if ______________________________.
   This is because ____.

3. Make up your own question: ____?
   What would have made ____________________ (better / worse) is ____________________ ______________________________________. This is because ______________________ ____.

Writing / Discussion:

I. What is something that you did in high school that you now regret?
   Back in high school, something that I regret is ____________________. This is because ____.

   What could you have done to make the situation either better or worse?
   What I could have done to make things (better / worse) is ______________________ ____.

   What type of counterfactual thinking is this? Why?
   It is (upward / downward, additive / subtractive) thinking. This is because __________ ____.

   Group Discussion: What advice do the others in your group have to offer?
   The counterfactual advice that the others in my group have to offer is ______________ ____.

II. What had been a major event in your life?
   A major event in my life is when I ______________________________. The reason is that ____ ____.

   What could you have done to make the situation either better or worse?
   What I should have done to make things (better / worse) is ______________________ ____.

   What type of thinking is this? Why?
   This is (upward / downward, additive / subtractive). This is because ______________ ____.

   Group Discussion: What advice do the others in your group have to offer?
   The counterfactual advice that the others in my group have to offer is ______________ ____.

Make up two questions of your own to discuss with the other class members. Be creative !!

20. Mindful Eating

Pre-Reading Question: What is mindful eating?

Vocabulary: Match the sentence beginnings with their endings.

1. automatically 自動的に	2. Buddhist 仏教徒	3. caress 触る
4. chew 吸収する	5. conscious 意識する	6. distractions 気を散らすもの
7. fully aware 十分に心得ている	8. utensils 用具	

1. She did her homework well and was **automatically** ____ a. the dangers of smoking.
2. As a **Buddhist**, he would ____ b. your food slowly and carefully.
3. The girl loved to **caress** her pet cat ____ c. rather than chopsticks.
4. It is important to **chew** ____ d. given the grade of A.
5. After the accident, he was fully **conscious** ____ e. she couldn't focus on her work.
6. With all the **distractions**, ____ f. pray at a temple every weekend.
7. Many students are not **fully aware** of ____ g. and aware of what happened.
8. Here, we use **utensils** such as spoons and forks ____ h. and listen to it purr.

21

"Mindfulness means paying attention in a particular way; on purpose, in the present moment, and nonjudgmentally." ***– Jon Kabat-Zinn, PhD***

[1] "Mindfulness" means being **fully aware** of everything around you, staying present in the moment, and being **conscious** of everything you are doing. The concept of mindful eating comes from **Buddhist** teachings. The goal is to connect us more deeply with the experience of eating. Buddhist teachers encourage students to eat in silence while sitting, breathing, and meditating. In one exercise, teachers give students some grapes or fruit to study and **caress** for 20 minutes. The goal is for students to notice everything about the food. In another exercise, people place a small amount of food in their mouth, but don't **chew** for 30 seconds. Most of us will never become Buddhist monks, of course, but there are plenty of ways to use these practices in everyday life.

[2] Unlike mindful eating, "mindless eating" means doing everything **automatically**, quickly putting food in your mouth without thinking or paying attention to what it is. People overall ignore the body's "hunger" signals and eat instead based on their current emotion – happy, sad, bored, lonely – or while doing something else (working, studying, watching TV), often stuffing their faces with junk food and fast food. Perhaps you, too often eat while rushing out the door, to work, or school. When you have a nice meal, the first bite is delicious, and the second bite is still good. Then you notice something on your smart phone or lap top but continue eating. Before you know it, all your food is gone. You wonder where it went. What were you thinking? After the meal, you feel as if you haven't even eaten. You are deeply disappointed. Maybe you will eat something more, but then you remember your promise to yourself to lose weight or eat better. The thing is, most of us do not even realize how mindlessly we eat our food until it is brought to our attention. Moving from mindless eating to mindful eating may be a simple idea, but it is much harder to put into practice than you think. It takes effort and patience.

[3] The purpose of mindful eating is to change your relationship with food. This goes beyond just thinking about what you are eating. Look at the food as if you have never seen or eaten it before. Consider how and where the food was grown and what farmer grew it. Basically, you are learning to pay attention and be present in the moment. What is important is not what you eat, but how to eat thoughtfully, purposely, mindfully. Take note of all the **distractions** around you (like your cell phone, music player, magazines, etc.) and remove them. Sit down, relax, and prepare to eat in silence. Look deeply into your meal and give it your full attention. Appreciate everything about it: look, smell, color, texture. Pause, take deep breaths, and begin. Take small bites and chew your food slowly, perhaps 20 times or more. Notice how each bite feels on your tongue. Experience chewing emotionally, tasting every part of the food, as long as possible from first bite to last. Close your eyes and focus on all that the food has to offer. Always be aware of all your feelings and emotions. What emotions does eating produce and how does the food make you feel? Pause and put down your **utensils** between bites. By acknowledging our food every few bites and breaths, we stop the habit of mindless eating. Have a hot or cold mindful drink. Pay attention to the food's quality, not its quantity. Appreciate the food more, and focus on the experience of eating and your meal's nutritional qualities.

[4] While eating mindfully, ask yourself, am I really hungry? Why am I eating? Eat when you are hungry, and stop when you are not. Eat with the goal of becoming healthy and improving well-being. Slow down and listen to the body's natural hunger signals. Where in the body do you feel the hunger? Feel the food as is moves in your stomach, and notice how your stomach feels as it gets fuller. How does your body feel before, during, and after eating? Keep focused on your body, noticing how you feel.

[5] When we eat too fast, we often overeat. This is because it takes the body about 20 minutes to realize that we're full. This knowledge is a powerful tool that will allow you to regain control of your eating. If you put in the time and succeed, you will naturally become more aware of your physical and emotional signals and better choose your food for its nutritional value and enjoyment. Research has shown that when you truly focus on the experience of eating, you enjoy the food more. You also eat less and make healthier food choices, which can help you lose weight and improve your health.

"Do, or do not. There is no try."

–Yoda

Active Outline: Choose the correct answer.

1. Mindful eating came from __________ teachings. (Christian / Japanese / Buddhist)
   a. In one exercise, people studied the food for 20 minutes __________ eating it. (before / while / after)
2. Mindless eating is __________. (automatic / thoughtful)
   a. Most people are used to __________ eating. (mindful / mindless)
   b. Changing from mindless to mindful eating __________ easy to do. (is / is not)
3. Mindful eating changes your relationship with your __________. (friends / parents / food / music)
   a. You must look at all distractions. (True / False)
   b. Chew the food __________. (slowly / quickly)
   c. You must pay attention to the food's __________. (quantity / quality)
4. It __________ important to listen to your body's natural hunger signals. (is / is not)
   a. Focus your attention on __________. (your eating / where you feel the hunger / Both of these.)
5. We often overeat when our eating is __________. (mindful / mindless)
   a. Other advantages of mindful eating include __________. (enjoying your food more / losing weight / better health / All of these.)

Comprehension: Write the number of the paragraph that the sentence best summarizes.

1. __4__ Discusses the importance of not eating when you are full.
2. __2__ Discusses how most people eat their food.
3. ____ Mentions that it takes at least 20 minutes to feel full.
4. ____ Explains that students keep food in their mouths without chewing for 30 seconds.
5. ____ Concludes that with mindful eating we eat less, and become healthier.
6. ____ Advises that you should pay attention to your body while eating.
7. ____ Discusses the importance of chewing slowly.
8. ____ Talks about exercises for Buddhist students on how to mindfully eat fruit.
9. ____ Shows ways in which people eat that makes them disappointed.
10. ____ Stresses the importance of focusing on the color, look, and smell of foods.

Understanding:

1. Name four times when you have eaten "mindlessly."
   a. ______________________________. b. ______________________________.
   c. ______________________________. d. ______________________________.
2. Give two reasons why mindful eating is not practical.
   a. ______________________________. b. ______________________________.
3. How could you better appreciate or value your food more?
   a. ______________________________. b. ______________________________.
   c. ______________________________. d. ______________________________.
4. Give three words to describe your current eating habits: (Ex: emotional, greedy, etc.)
   1. ____________________ 2. ____________________ 3. ____________________

Critical Thinking: What parts of today's reading do you agree with? What parts do you disagree with?

Agree:
1.
2.

Disagree:
1.
2.

Opinion: Overall, do you agree or disagree with the ideas presented in the article? Why?

Assignment: Do a mindful eating exercise. Then complete the writing exercise below.

When I tried my mindful eating exercise for the first time, what happened was

____

______________________________.

I did it on the day of ______________ for (breakfast / lunch / dinner / __________).

What I noticed about the food's flavors, smell, etc. was ______________________.

Compared to my usual experience of eating, it was ______________________

______________________________.

I (do / do not) believe that mindful eating gives more satisfaction while eating. This is because ______________________________.

I also (do / do not) believe that mindful eating assists in healthier eating. This is because

______________________________.

Writing / Discussion: Describe your eating habits and behavior. How do you eat? Do you eat quickly or slowly? Do you eat too little, too much, or just what you are given or is in the package? Explain.

____

____

____

Debate: What do you think of mindful eating? Can mindful eating really change your relationship with food? Why or why not? Discuss this question with your classmates.

Make up two questions of your own to discuss with the other class members. Be creative !!

21. The Id, Ego, and Superego

Pre-Question: What are the id, the ego, and the superego?

Vocabulary: Match the words with their meanings or descriptions

1. compromise 妥協する	2. conflict 対立する	3. conscience 良心
4. overlap 重複する	5. primitive 根源的な	

____ a. Old and very simple
____ b. A fight or disagreement
____ c. To try and come to an agreement
____ d. Our sense of right and wrong
____ e. To cover a part of something

CD 22

"Knowing yourself is the beginning of all wisdom."
– Aristotle

[1] No one in history did more to advance the field of psychology than Sigmund Freud. In the early 1900s, he tried to explain how personalities develop and how the mind itself works. He believed that people did not control their mind directly, but were actually controlled by what he called the id, the ego, and the superego, and that these three personality "agents" are in **conflict** with one another. This conflict, Freud said, helps to explain people's complex behavior.

[2] The Id: The id develops when we are born. It is where our most **primitive** desires are located, a part of the mind that cannot be directly controlled. The id consists of our basic needs, wants, and urges. It is selfish, unreasonable, and demands that everything be done right now. The id does not understand good, evil, or morals. It does not care about other people or anything outside of itself. Its only desire is to increase pleasure. Children are completely controlled by the id. They cry when they get hungry and demand food right now. They don't care if their parents are busy or relaxing or sleeping. But the id itself is not "bad" or "evil." When we reach adulthood, the id becomes an important part of us. It is our jealousy and greed, and enjoys power, control, and aggression. It is why adults smoke, drink alcohol, gossip, and hurt others. But without the id, people would be rather boring. The id creates our reason for living, our wants and drives—and where would we be without those? For example, it is behind our drive to succeed, do well in sports, get a better job, accomplish more, want nicer things, compete harder, and achieve our goals. So in a way, our id helps us survive.

[3] The Ego: This is the second "agent" of the personality, and develops around the age of three. Its most important job is to **compromise**, between the two other parts of the personality. To do this, the ego makes plans for solving problems. If the id says it's thirsty, for example, the ego finds a way to get a drink. If the id is angry, the ego works to solve the problem, if possible, without hurting others. Like the id, the ego does not understand feelings, morals, right and wrong. It does not seek pleasure. It is concerned with how we relate to other people. While the ego wants to satisfy the id, it knows that the id's selfishness will cause us trouble in the long run.

[4] The Superego: This is the third part of the personality that develops around the age of five. It is judgmental, concerned with moral rules, right and wrong. It works in two ways. 1. It wants us to become the best person we can be, and when we are not our best, the superego gives us feelings of guilt, worry, and shame to make us aim higher. Moreover, when we behave properly, it rewards us with feelings of great pride. 2. It acts like our **conscience** and demands that we behave morally toward others and in society. The superego helps us make "correct" decisions, wants us to study harder, help others, do our best work, and become the best person we can be. It is in a constant battle with the id and demands that the ego control it.

[5] Freud believed that the id, the ego, and the superego are not actual parts of the brain – they are ideas or concepts. There is no clear separation between them; they **overlap**. In a healthy person, the ego must be the strongest "agent." It has a difficult job to do, because it must work out compromises between the primitive desires of the id and the righteous judgements of the superego. If our id is too weak, Freud said, we will suffer depression, stress, or other emotional afflictions. If it is too strong, we might act out on our feelings and anger, bully others, and maybe even commit crimes. If the superego is too weak, we might do things only for pleasure, without feeling guilt, maybe with a total loss of personal control. If the superego is too strong, we can become very rigid and inflexible, follow too many rules too closely, demand too much from others, be judgmental and perfectionist, and not accept others whom we consider "bad" or "immoral."

"Be master of mind rather than mastered by mind."
– Zen Proverb

Active Outline: Choose the correct answer.

1. Sigmund Freud believed that people __________ directly control their minds. (do / do not)
   a. The three parts of our personality are in __________ with one another. (conflict / agreement)
2. The id is formed when we are __________. (born / three years old / five years old).
   a. The id __________. (is greedy / likes pleasure / is demanding / All of these.)
3. The ego works mostly to __________. (be selfish / judge people / compromise)
   a The ego __________ understand right and wrong. (does / does not)
4. The superego gives us feelings of __________. (guilt / worry / pride / All of these.)
   a. The superego is in conflict with __________. (the id / the ego / itself)
5. The id, the ego, and the superego __________ actual physical parts of the brain. (are / are not)
   a. The __________ must be the strongest for the person to be healthy. (id / ego / superego)
   b. If the __________ is too strong, the person gets angry easily. (id / ego / superego)
   c. If the __________ is too strong, the person is overly judgmental of others. (id / ego / superego)

Comprehension: Put an "X" next to the correct answer. (There may be more than one correct answer).

1. "I don't understand right and wrong."	id ___	ego ___	superego ___
2. "I need to figure out how to solve this."	id ___	ego ___	superego ___
3. "I can do a better job."	id ___	ego___	superego ___
4. "We fight with each other constantly."	id ___	ego ___	superego___
5. "I am so sorry."	id ___	ego ___	superego___
6. "Let's compromise."	id ___	ego ___	superego ___
7. "I want more."	id ___	ego ___	superego ___

Word Fill: Decide whether the statements represent the id (ID), the ego (EGO), or the superego (SE).

1. I want it now. ID We must compromise. EGO This is not moral. SE
2. A child is demanding candy. ___ Your younger sister is eating ice cream, and you take it. ___
3. You study instead of going to a party. ___
   You "borrow" your mother's necklace without telling her. ___
4. You return a ring you found instead of keeping it. ___
   I could not help buying the gold ring. ___
5. You cheat on a test. ___ You do not cheat, even though you could. ___
   Let's make a deal. ___
6. You are rude to another person. ___ You feel regret after being rude. ___
7. You decide not to gossip to others. ___ I feel so guilty. ___
8. You save a dog, despite danger to yourself. ___ I want nicer shoes. ___
9. You find 100,000 yen: You take it. ___ You turn it in. ___ You turn it in to get a reward. ___
10. You do not steal, because you could get caught. ___
    You do not steal, because it is wrong. ___
11. You want to lose weight: You have a piece of pie. ___ You have a salad. ___
12. Your mother made a cake: You eat it all. ___ You just have one slice. ___
    You leave it for later. ___
13. You visit a friend and see a last cookie: You eat it when he isn't looking. ___
    You leave it there. ___ You share it. ___
14. You are in class and thirsty: You leave to get a drink. ___
    You wait for class to end and find a water fountain. ___

Creative Thinking: Create your own examples of id, ego, and superego statements.

Id: 1. ____________________ 2. ____________________
Ego: 1. ____________________ 2. ____________________
Superego: 1. ____________________ 2. ____________________

Sentence Completion: Fill in the blanks with id, ego, or superego.

When I was very young, I would become very angry with my big brother. I would often cry, or even throw things at him. The (1) __________ was in complete control of me. I believed that acting out physically was the only way to act. As I got older, I learned to compromise, and told my brother why I was so unhappy. In other words, I stopped acting so childishly. My (2) __________ was developing. One day, my brother needed help with his bicycle. We worked together to fix it, and it gave me a great feeling of success and satisfaction. My (3) __________ had developed!

At school, my brother's friend got a new haircut. Some other students started making fun of him. Their (4) __________ was acting out. For the next few days, the boy wore a hat. His (5) __________ had found a solution to the bullying problem. We helped by telling the other students that we thought his hair and hat looked nice, and the bullying soon stopped. Our (6) __________ had allowed us to help others.

Individual Role Play: In this role play, you play the roles of the id, the ego, and the superego.

You go to the store. Your id says: ____.

Your superego says: ____.

Your ego makes a compromise decision: ____.

Group Role Play: In a small group, one person takes the role of the id, another plays the ego, and one more person is the superego. First, plan / write your role-play "script" by filling in the blanks below. Then, when you act out the role play, keep it going for a few minutes by "ad-libbing." ***Be creative. Have fun!!***

You go to ____________________. The id says: ____________________.

The superego says: ____.

The ego decides: ____.

Short Answers:

1. Name a time when you saw another person's id in complete control.
   A time when I saw another person's id in control was when ____________________
   ____.
2. Name a time when your ego made a decision for you.
   A time that I had a decision to make, and my ego decided for me was when __________
   ____.
3. Name a time when your superego made you feel worried or guilty.
   A time when my superego made me feel (worried / guilty) was when __________
   ____.

Questions / Discussions:

I. When has your id taken over, and given you the out-of-control urge to do something?
   A time when an urge has taken me over, and I just had to (do / have) something was when ______________________________ *What happened was*
   ____.

II. When did you and your ego have a difficult decision to make or problem to solve?
   A time when I had a (difficult decision to make / problem to solve) was when __________
   __________. *What happened was* ______________________________.

III. When did you and your superego want you to become your best self?
   A time when I wanted to become my best self was when, ____________________
   ____.
   What happened was ______________________________
   ____.

Debate: Do you think Freud's theory of the id, the ego, and the superego is true? Is it interesting? Is it useful? Why or why not? Discuss this question with your classmates.

Make up two questions of your own to discuss with the other class members. Be creative !!

Listing of Vocabulary

	Vocabulary Word	Japanese	SKT
1. Cat Café			
	companionship	交わり	「カムペアネィアンシュイップ」
	cuddle	寄り添う	「カドウ」
	judge	判断する	「ヂュアヂュ」
	self-esteem	自尊心	「スエウ゜スティーム」
	sociable	社交的な	「ソゥシュアブウ」
	themes	テーマ、主題	「スイーム」
2. Sad Songs			
	chills	寒気	「チュイウ（ズ）」
	cope with	対抗する	「コウプ　ウィズ」
	empathy	共感	「エンパスイ」
	journey	旅	「ヂュア～ネィ」
	overcame	乗り越える	「オゥヴァケィム」
	nostalgic	郷愁に満ちた	「ナステァウヂュク」
	substance	物質	「サブスタンス」
3. The History of Consumerism			
	controls demand	需要を制御する	「カントロウズ　ディマンド」
	consumer culture	消費者文化	「カンスウマァ　カウチュア」
	defined	定義する	「ディウ゜ァインド」
	overwhelmed	圧倒する	「オゥヴァヘウムド」
	status	地位	「スティタス」
	store credit	支払ったお金を返金せずお店に預けておくこと	「ストーァ　クレディト」
4. A Sense of Purpose			
	big picture	大局	「ビイグ　ピクチュア」
	confidence	自信	「カンウ゜ァダンス」
	donate	寄付する	「ドゥネィティング」
	flexible	柔軟な	「ウ゜ヌレクスィブゥ」
	inspiration	刺激	「インスパレイシュンヌ」
	meaningful relationships	有意義な関係	「ミーネィグウ゜ウ　レリヌレィシュンシィプス」
	psychological	心理的な	「サィコヌラーヂュカウ」
5. Santa Claus			
	chimneys	煙突	「チュイムネィズ」
	elf	妖精	「エウウ゜」
	elves	妖精（複数）	「エウヴズ」
	fur trim	毛皮の飾り付きの	「ウ゜ゥラ　チュイム」
	huge feasts	盛大な祝宴	「ヒェュヂュ　ウ゜ースツ」
	nodded	頷く	「ナーディング」
	puppet	操り人形	「パペット」
	sleigh	そり	「スヌレィ」
	sneaky	こっそりとする	「スネィーキィ」
	statue	像	「ステアチュウ」

	Vocabulary Word	Japanese	SKT
6. The Same-Sex Wedding			
	certificate	証明書	「セァ～テェウ゜イキト」
	civil partnership	市民パートナーシップ	「スィヴィウ　パーァトナァシュイップ」
	gay	同性愛者	「ゲィ」
	politician	政治家	「パーヌラティシュンヌ」
	slight majority	少しだけの多数派	「サィヌレント　マヂョーラティ」
	symbolic	象徴的な	「スイムバーヌリク」
	uncomfortable	居心地の悪い	「アヌカンウ゜ヌブウ」
7. World Festivals			
	afterlife	死後の生活	「ェアウ゜タァラヌイウ゜」
	bullfighting	闘牛	「ブウウ゜アィティング」
	bulls	雄牛	「ブゥウ（ズ）」
	haunted house	お化け屋敷	「ホーンティドハウス」
	Lent	四旬節（レント）	「レヌント」
	leprechauns	レプラカーン（伝説の妖精）	[レヌプラコアコーァンヌ]
	pinch	傷つける	「ピンチュ」
	skeletons	骸骨	「スケーラヌタンズ」
	souls	魂	「スウォウズ」
8. What Makes You Happier:Experiences or Luxury Goods			
	basic needs are met	基本的欲求が満たされる	「ベイスィクネィーヅ　アーメート」
	envy	ねたみ	「エンヴィ」
	fade	徐々に消え去る	「ウ゜ェイド」
	frustrated	いらいらする	「ウ゜ゥラスチュエイティド」
	remodeling	改築	「ゥリマードリング」
	souvenirs	土産	「スウヴェネィァ（ズ）」
9. Teenagers and Stress			
	fitting in	溶け込む	「ウィティングインヌ」
	manage	制御する	「マエナネヂュ」
	miserable	惨めな	「ミゼラブウ」
	motivates	動機付ける	「モゥティヴェイツ」
	nap	昼寝	「ネアプ」
	pressure	プレッシャー	「プゥレシュァ」
	procrastinating	先延ばしにすること	「プヌロクサスネエィティイング」
	teased	いじめられる	「ティーズド」
10. Superheroes			
	accident-prone nerd	事故を起こしやすいオタク	「アクデントープロウンヌ～ド」
	awkward	不器用な	「オークァァド」
	bullied	いじめた	「ブヌリード」
	clay	粘土	「クヌレィ」
	craze	流行	「クウレイズ」
	golden lasso	金の投げ縄	「ゴゥウデン　ヌラアソウ」
	x-ray vision	X 線視覚（透視能力）	「エークスレィヴィジュンヌ」

	Vocabulary Word	Japanese	SKT
11. Gratitude			
	appreciate	感謝する	「アプリースィエイト」
	depression	落ち込み	「ディプレーシュンヌ」
	expressing	表現する	「イクプレッスイング」
	materialistic	物質的	「マティアリヌリスティク」
	opposite	反対の	「アーパズイト」
	philosophy	哲学	「ウ゜ィラヌーサウ゜ィ」
	properly	適切に	「プウロペァヌリィ」
12. Processed Foods and Addiction			
	addictive	中毒性のある	「エアディクティヴ」
	chemicals	化学物質	「ケミクウズ」
	crave	強く望む	「クゥレエイヴ」
	grease	油脂	「グリーズ」
	narcotics	麻薬	「ナーアカーティクス」
	overeat	食べ過ぎる	「オゥヴァイート」
	processed foods	加工食品	「プロセスト　ウ゜ウヅ」
	rotting	腐敗すること	「ラーティング」
	texture	質感	「テークスクチュア」
13. Minimalism			
	clutter	がらくたの山	「クヌラタア」
	decluttering	片づけ	「デクヌラタアング」
	distracting	目をそらさせる	「ディスラクティング」
	frustration	不満	「ウッラスチュレイシュンヌ」
	miserable	悲惨な	「ミゼラブウ」
	possessions	所有物	「ポゼーズエーシュンズ」
	society	社会	「ソゥサイアティ」
14. Flow			
	boredom	退屈	「ボーアドム」
	distractions	気を散らすもの	「ディスチュエアクシュンズ」
	effortless	楽に	「エウ゜アトヌレエス」
	enthusiasm	熱意	「インスゥウズイアズム」
	involved	関わりを持つ	「インヴァーヴド」
	passive	受け身で	「ペアスィヴ」
	wander	彷徨い歩く	「ワーンダア」
15. The Benefits of Being Scared			
	chemical	化学的な	「ケミカウ」
	confident	自信に満ちた	「カーンウ゜ィダント」
	criticized	批判された	「クリティサイズド」
	explore	探検する	「イクスプヌローア」
	expose	さらす	「イクスポゥズ」
	immune system	免疫システム	「イミュウンヌ　スィステム」
	nightmares	悪夢	「ナイトメアズ」

16. Social Media and the Fear of Missing Out (FoMO)

Vocabulary Word	Japanese	SKT
brag	威張る、誇示する	「ブゥレアグ」
compare	比較する	「カアンペァ」
compete	競う	「カムピィーㇳ」
concentrate	集中する	「カーンセントレイㇳ」
idealized	理想化された	「アィディアヌライズド」
unintentionally	意図しないで	「アンネンシュナリヌリィ」

17. Gender Neutral Parenting

Vocabulary Word	Japanese	SKT
advertisements	広告	「ェデヴァエアタィズマンツ」
evolution	進化	「エヴァルウシュン[ヌ]」
diapers	おむつ	「ダィアパァズ」
nurturing	育てること	「ナァ～チュアリング」
pregnant	妊娠して	「プレウグナンㇳ」
stereotyping	ステレオタイプ	「ステゥレオゥタィピング」

18. The Science of Altruism

Vocabulary Word	Japanese	SKT
altruism	利他主義	「エアウチュイズウズム」
empathy	共感	「エムパㇲイ」
human evolution	人間の進化	「ヒューマン⌒ネヴァヌルウシュン[ヌ]」
reputation	評判	「ゥレピュティシュンヌ」
spouse	結婚の相手	「スパゥズ」
trust	信頼	「トゥラスㇳ」

19. Counterfactual Thinking

Vocabulary Word	Japanese	SKT
compare	比較する	「カンペァ」
consider	考える	「カンスイダァ」
disappointment	落胆	「ディサポイントマンㇳ」
expected	予想した	「イクスペㇰティド」
scientists	科学者たち	「サィァンティスツ」

20. Mindful Eating

Vocabulary Word	Japanese	SKT
automatically	自動的に	「アートメアティカヌリィ」
Buddhist	仏教徒	「ブデイスッ」
caress	触る	「カゥレース」
chew	吸収する	「チュゥウ」
distractions	気を散らすもの	「ディスチュェアㇰシュンズ」
fully aware	十分に心得ている	「ウ゚ィリヌイ　アウエァ」
utensils	用具	「ユユテエンスィウズ」

21. The Id, Ego, and Superego

Vocabulary Word	Japanese	SKT
compromise	妥協する	「カムプロマィズ」
conflict	対立する	「カーンリウ゚ヌクㇳ」
conscience	良心	「カーンシャス」
overlap	重複する	「オゥヴァレェアヌプ」
primitive	根源的な	「プリマティヴ」

SKT とは（解説）

「カナ表記」の名称は誤解されやすいのでSKTと言っています。それはShimaoka Kana Transcriptionの頭字語です。

I 1. 母音：

ant	luck	ma	heat	hit	tool	book	bed	day	ball	coat
[æ]	[ʌ]	[ɑː]	[iː]	[i]	[uː]	[ʊ]	[e]	[eɪ]	[ɔː]	[oʊ]
ェア	ア	アー	イー	イェ	ゥウ	ウォ	エ	エィ	オー	オゥ

（簡略記号3種：イ　ウー　ウ）

特殊な母音：[əːr] ＝「**エ〜**ァ」例：**bird** [bəːrd]「**べ〜**ァド」鳥（米語発音）

2. 文字の太い / 細い で、強 / 弱を表し、大きい／小さい で , 音実質を表す。

例：psychology「サィ**カー**ヌラヂュイ」心理学 (米語発音)

3. 弱母音　[ァ、ゥ ＝ ə]　例：**Japan**「ヂュ**ペア**ンヌ」日本

「ァ」は曖昧音、または、母音の後の r 音

II. 4. 子音　重要な区別：

l と r：l 音は舌先側音性の特徴から、「ヌル」で表す。

r 音は下唇の円唇の特徴から、「ゥル」で表す。

例：**light**「**ヌラ**ィト」／ **right**「**ゥラ**ィト」

th と s, z：th は両唇間—舌先音なので舌先−歯茎音の s、z より弱い。

例：**think**「ス**イ**ンク」／ **sink**「**スィ**ンク」

then「ズ**エ**ンヌ」／ **Zen**「**ズエ**ンヌ」

5. tr-, dr- などの子音連結：

tr-：try「チュアィ」（円唇）英音では「tr ⇒ tʃ」で発音する。

dr-：dream「ヂュイーム」英音では「dr」（円唇）⇒「dʒ」で発音する。

6. 円唇音など：

wind「ゥ**ウィ**ンド」　**change**「**チュエィ**ンヂュ」　**money**「**マ**ネィ」

judge「**ヂュア**ヂュ」　**teacher**「**ティー**チュァ」　**English**「**イ**ングヌリシュ」

share「**シュエ**ァ」　**usually**「**ユウ**ジュァヌリィ」　**tennis**「**テー**ネィス」

7. 補注： 1. 小さい「ュ」は円唇を示す。

2.「ヌル」左肩文字は r 音と異なり、舌の側面が上歯と接することを示す。

3.「ンヌ」右肩文字は鼻濁音で口からの通路が完全に遮断されることを示す。

4. p, b; t, d; k, g など小さい細字は弱いか聞こえないかを示す。